PRESBYTERIA
VOLUME ONE

BIBLICAL CHURCH GOVERNMENT

by Don K. Clements

Metokos Press
Narrows, VA 24124

Presbyterian Primers: Volume 1
Biblical Church Government

Published by Metokos Press, an affiliate of Metokos Ministries,
a parachurch ministry providing 'Encouragement For Small
Churches'. Visit us on the web at www.metokos.org

Cover design by Chip Evans, Walker-Atlanta
Printed in the United States by Walker Printing, Montgomery Alabama

ISBN 0-9742331-0-2

Presbyterian Primers is intended as a brief series of medium length books written in a non-academic style which (hopefully) will be accessible to the many people (but especially 'guys') in churches who do not regularly read books about 'church stuff.'

Since my seminary days I have frequently complained that in arenas other than Reformed and Presbyterian circles, one could find many books written in such a manner, but the majority of Reformed and Presbyterian related works were either designed as Adult Sunday School textbooks (with the expectation of a certain level of understanding that goes with such readers) or were written by academics with the hope that fellow academics and a few academically-minded people would buy enough copies to cover the cost of publication. There has seldom been literature designed more specifically to reach young or previously unread church members on topics of importance.

The series will have at least three volumes (and, if there appears to be a desire and market), several more. After this volume on Church Government it is my intention to write on Church History (pointed towards evangelical American Presbyterian denominations) and one yet untitled on the essentials of faith (I would shy away from the word doctrine) that members (rather than officers) of an evangelical Presbyterian congregation could benefit from reading.

BIBLICAL CHURCH GOVERNMENT

Volume One of the Presbyterian Primers series is on the topic of Church Government not because that is the most important topic for people new to church life or early in their spiritual development (although an argument could be made for that view). Rather it is the topic for which I was furthest along in developing a manuscript to publish.

A quick read through the Acknowledgments will show the number of years and various venues in which I have been engaged in the study of and teaching of this topic.

And while this will become crystal clear during the reading of the book, it's worth saying here that my personal commitment to the Presbyterian form of government caused me to put this much work into this topic. The work was not only in the study and teaching of the topic, but also in the practice of Church Government at the local, Presbytery and General Assembly level.

By God's grace I have been honored to serve as Stated Clerk of Mid Atlantic, New River, and Blue Ridge Presbyteries of the PCA, as well as serving as a member of denominational-level committees for more than 20 years – including three years on an Ad-Interim Study Committee which tackled the question dealt with in Chapter Four – "How Many Offices Are There In the Church?" It is my hope that this experience has seasoned this work with a helpful practicality.

ACKNOWLEDGEMENTS

Since it would be impossible to develop this list in order of importance and influence, I have chosen to do it chronologically.

While it should go without saying, it is always worth saying — Soli Deo Gloria!

To my wife Esther, who has listened to this material in sermons, Sunday School classes, Bible studies, and on video more times than she would care to count.

To the Session of Perry Presbyterian Church, Perry, Georgia who, during the summer of 1972, helped a young seminary student-intern learn what it means for the people of God to confirm gifts for the ministry from a young man who had many doubts.

To Dr. George Knight, a dear friend as well as my New Testament mentor and academic guide through the principals of Church Government while I was at Covenant Seminary and who initially drew my interest to the 'Two-Office – Three Office' controversy.

To the Session and congregation at Eastern Heights Presbyterian Church in Savannah, Georgia who provided the initial crucible for me to put academic theory into practice for the first time—not always with great success.

My fellow committee members on the PCA Ad Interim Committee to Study the Number of Offices in the Church from 1974 through 1977 who provided much iron to sharpen my newly acquired iron of understanding the issues at stake.

To the students in the Adult Sunday School at New Covenant Presbyterian Church, Virginia Beach, Virginia who during the 1980-83 church years were first introduced to the 'Presbyterian Primers' concept, including the material in this book.

To Dr. Carl Saylor, Director of the DMin program at Gordon Conwell Theological Seminary in the mid 80's (during which time my fellow students and I referred to the program as the 'Best DMin Program in America from which no one will ever graduate!), along with the late Dr. Elmer Smick, my advisor at GCTS, both of whom helped to mold the thesis project from which this book is drawn.

To Marvin Padgett, Vice President (Editorial) at Crossway Books, who—while recognizing the market for this series and book was two narrow for his company to publish—considered the concept important enough to encourage me to keep searching until I could find a publisher.

To Dr. Susannah Clements, Assistant Professor of English at the University of Sioux Falls, SD, for her professional assistance in editing the manuscript. (Yes, she is the author's daughter, who along with sisters Stephanie and Sarah (Hein) who have always been a *'delight to my heart.'*

Narrows, Virginia
May 2003

TABLE OF CONTENTS

BIBLICAL CHURCH GOVERNMENT

CHAPTER 1

The Importance Of Leadership

As we begin this book, let me first present something that in marketing is frequently called "the hook." My purpose in this chapter is to try to get your attention – to try to convince you that this topic is absolutely essential, both to you as an individual Christian and particularly to your church.

It is true that there are many things that are important to you and to me in our individual Christian lives – in spiritual matters which affect us as individuals, such as our salvation, our assurance, our growth in grace. But Christians are not merely individuals. They are also united together in one body – the glorious body of Christ, the church. And so in the church, in the corporate life of believers, there is nothing more important than its leadership. As the leadership goes, so goes the church. It can be no other way, for that is exactly how God intended it to be.

Recall some important events in Biblical history with me for a moment, and you will see clearly that leadership is the key to either God's blessing or to God's curse upon his people. You see, when God had some special blessing for his people, he gave them a leader or, in some cases, several leaders.

Think of the leadership exercised by Abraham, in directing his very large family according to the teachings of God. Think of the combined leadership of Moses and Aaron and the elders of Israel in guiding and directing the people of God for many difficult years. Think of the leadership exercised by Joshua and the godly judges of Israel in the Promised Land. But then think of the lack of leadership Israel so often suffered during that same period.

In Judges, Chapter 2, we find the children of Israel having completed their conquest of the Promised Land under the leadership of Joshua. Beginning at verse 6, the author writes: *"When Joshua dismissed the people, the people of Israel went each to his inheritance to take possession of the land. [7] And the people served the Lord all the days of Joshua, and all the days of the elders who outlived Joshua, who had seen all the great work that the Lord had done for Israel."*

We see here the effect of godly leadership. Fruitful lives for the people of God. But then the story continues in verse 8: *"And Joshua the son of Nun, the servant of the Lord, died at the age of 110 years."* The great leader God had given to his people passed from the scene. And shortly after that, the elders with him had passed. The story continues in verses 10 and 11: *"And all that generation also were gathered to their fathers. And there arose another generation after them who did not know the Lord or the work that he had done for Israel. And the people of Israel did what was evil in the sight of the Lord and served the Baals. "*

It is not necessary to review all the evil and sin that they did, but clearly you see that the people, left without godly leadership, did not follow the teachings of God. And what was God's answer to this problem of wicked disobedience? We see this in verses 16 through 19: *"Then the Lord raised up judges, who saved them out of the hand of those who plundered them. Yet they did not listen to their judges, for they whored after other gods and bowed down to them. They soon turned aside from the way in which their fathers had walked, who had obeyed the commandments of the Lord, and they did not do so. Whenever the Lord raised up judges for them, the Lord was with the judge, and he saved them from the hand of their enemies all the days of the judge. For the Lord was moved to pity by their groaning because of those who afflicted and oppressed them. But whenever the judge died, they turned back and were more corrupt than their fathers, going after other gods, serving them and bowing down to them. They did not drop any of their practices or their stubborn ways."*

It is important to see what this passage is teaching us today. That when there are no leaders, when there is a leadership crisis in the church, the people are left to their own devices, and the end is always, always corruption, disobedience, and sin. Over and over again you see, written by God for our instruction in his word, the sad tale, repeated several times for us throughout this book: *"In those days there was no king in Israel. Everyone did what was right in his own eyes"* (Judges 17:6). God's people without a leader did whatever they, as individuals, thought was right. Mob rule. Anarchy at its worst. Because there was a crisis in leadership.

But God loved his people, and so he gave them a great leader – perhaps one of the greatest leaders in all the history of the world – King David. And we know, of course, of the history of Israel after David. When there was a good king and when there was sound, Biblical, godly leadership in the nation, then there was revival and joy and peace. But when there was an evil king, when there was weak or poor or ungodly leadership, then there were problems. To such a degree, finally, that the children of Israel ended up in captivity in Babylon.

We also see the same pattern repeated in the New Testament. God used leaders to bring about his plan. Jesus came to earth and gathered to Himself twelve leaders – his immediate disciples. And much of the message of the Gospels deals with the issue of leadership training, of Jesus teaching his disciples how to carry out his will.

The same thing is true in the early church, in the book of Acts and in the writings of Paul. Has it ever occurred to you how much of those books is about leaders or is addressed to leaders? The whole Bible is, in one sense, a manual of leadership training. That is the pattern of Biblical history. When God's people prospered and when the church was in true revival, it was because God gave his people great leaders.

The same thing is true yet today. Your church, my church, any church is only as good as its leaders. Leadership is clearly a gift from God. God gives his church leaders to rule and to govern and to guide and to care for his people. We can see this spelled out in the 4th Chapter of Ephesians. In this chapter, as in all of the book, Paul is concerned with unity in the church. Verse 3: *"[be] eager to maintain the unity of the Spirit in the bond of peace."* Paul wanted to keep unity and peace in the church.

But Paul knew how God would have that unity and peace kept. Not by some man-made ethical principles of whatever we think is best in our eyes. Rather, at verse 7 he speaks of the way in which this is to be done in the church: *"But grace was given to each one of us according to the measure of Christ's gift."* We understand that God's grace is the way he provides for our needs. And that grace is given by Jesus Himself to his church.

One important thing to note here is something that you cannot see while you are reading English translations of the Bible. There is a word in verse 7 that most translations render as *"gift."* The New International Version (NIV) calls it *"apportionment,"* which is a bit closer to the root meaning, but most others, including the ESV, call it "gift." This is not the same word that appears in many other places in the New Testament also as the English word "gift," such as in the lists of charismatic gifts in Romans 12, 1 Corinthians 12, and 1 Corinthians 14. Those are indeed gifts, even gifts of the Spirit. But this is a different word here in Ephesians 4. This is *"Christ's gift."*

In order to understand this gift, we have to look at a passage in the Gospel of Matthew. In Chapter 7, in the middle of the Sermon on the Mount, Jesus is speaking. Beginning at verse 7, he is teaching about prayer: *"Ask and it will be given you."* And as he continues, he gives an illustration, beginning at verse 9: *"Or which one of you, if his son asks him for bread, will give him a stone? Or if he asks for a fish, will give him a serpent? If you then, who are evil, know how to give good gifts to your children, how much more will your Father who is in heaven give good things to those who ask him!"* (9-11)

The word in verse 11, which is translated "gift," is the same Greek word that appears back in Ephesians 4. These are the only two places in the Bible where that particular Greek word occurs. And so it leads us to understand that this is a very special kind of gift. It is not the sort of gift that is like a present you get on your birthday. It is not something extra, something special, something nice that you are happy you have and you can use, and it is good and all that. It is not that kind of gift. That is what a charismatic gift is.

Rather, this gift in Matthew 7 is something that cannot be done without. It is something that is absolutely necessary. A child cannot live – cannot exist – without the bread and meat his father is to give him. He must have it for existence. It is not something nice, something extra, something pleasant you can take or leave. It is an absolute necessity.

With this understanding of the word in question, as we examine Ephesians 4, again we find the same sort of necessity for life. Only this time it is to the church that this gift is given. It is to the people of God that Jesus is giving something that they cannot live without. And what is that gift?

Well, verse 8 is a quote from the Old Testament, by which Paul shows that the finished work of Christ, described in the New Testament, is a fulfillment of the prophecy of the Old Testament. And then verses 9 and 10 are his commentary on that verse. The verse is a quote from Psalm 68, and Paul is saying that Jesus has fulfilled the promise of that Psalm.

But in verse 11 we now find out what the gift – what the apportionment – is that the church must have in order to exist. *"And he gave the apostles, the prophets, the evangelists, the pastors and teachers . . ."* If you use the KJV or others like it, the punctuation might throw you off. You may know that in the

16

original languages of the Bible there was no punctuation. So commas and semicolons and so on in the translations are not inspired. The correct punctuation is as the ESV gives it, with their use of what the editorial guru's tell me is called the 'Harvard Comma', clearly indicating there are only four groups in the context, with the final group called 'Pastors and Teachers." It would probably be even better to show it as a hyphenated term (Pastor-Teacher).

There are four groups of gifts here. Four different types of leaders that Jesus gave to his church for a very special reason. Apostles. Prophets. Evangelists. Pastor-Teachers. And what was the special reason Jesus gave these leaders to the church? The next verse, verse 12, contains the answer to that question: *"...to equip the saints for the work of ministry, for building up the body of Christ . . ."*

Of course that body of Christ is his church here on earth. Christ, the ascended Lord, gave necessary gifts – gave an appor-tionment to the church – in the form of leadership. The church could no more have existed without apostles, without prophets, without evangelists, and without pastor-teachers than a son could exist without the provision by his father of bread and meat to eat.

Leadership in the church of Jesus Christ is not an option. It is an absolute necessity. It is something that the church must have, something the church cannot live without. God deliver us from ever ending up as the children of Israel did in the days when there were no leaders and everyone did their own thing – doing whatever they decided was best in their own eyes.

And so this book is far more than just a series of Bible studies. This book deals with a topic that is crucial to the church of Christ – the subject of leadership. So crucial that the very life and health and existence of your own church, of any church, are dependent on what happens to its leadership.

Now, how should we go about our study? What should be our guideline? Should we get out some Book of Church Order and study it? Do we see how the Presbyterian Church in America or the Presbyterian Church in Scotland is governed? Do we see how the Baptist, or the Lutheran, or the Episcopal – or any church, for that matter – is governed? No, not at all! We have only one textbook to study, and that is the Bible. The Scriptures must be our guide.

And again on this point we really have no options. Not that some Christians won't disagree on this point. Some would even say: "Whatever works is fine. The Bible doesn't really give many specifics, so let's just do whatever works for us and that will be OK." But this must never be our view. It can only lead us to the disastrous condemnation that we are doing whatever seems right in our own eyes, and this is the condemnation of a church without leadership.

The Bible must (always!) be our primary directive in the study of church government and leadership. We want now to examine a couple of pertinent passages of the Bible to see why this is indeed the case.

First we want to look at 1 Corinthians, Chapter 3. In verse 5 we begin to see the context of the passage. *"What then is Apollos?*

What is Paul? Servants through whom you believed . . ." You see, Paul is here talking about leadership in the church. He continues at verse 7: *"So neither he who plants nor he who waters is anything, but only God who gives the growth."* Continuing at verse 9: *"For we are God's fellow workers. You are God's field, God's building."* It is clear that Paul is talking about the church, the body of Christ. Verse 10: *"According to the grace of God given to me, like a skilled master builder I laid a foundation, and someone else is building upon it. Let each one take care how he builds upon it."*

We want to pause here to understand this important phrase we have just read. Paul is saying that each one should be careful how he builds upon the foundation of the church of Jesus Christ. How we build in the church – that is, how leadership is carried out – is going to matter a great deal.

Continuing now at verse 11: *"For no one can lay a foundation other than that which is laid, which is Jesus Christ. [12] Now if anyone builds on the foundation with gold, silver, precious stones . . ."* Here Paul breaks his train of thought, and then carries right on in a slightly different frame of reference: *". . . wood, hay, or straw."* In other words, the foundation is gold, silver, and precious stones. That's what Jesus Christ really is. And we cannot be building on that foundation with wood, hay, and straw. We must take heed how we build, how we exercise leadership. Why? The answer is in verse 13: *". . . each one's work will become manifest, for the Day will disclose it, because it will be revealed by fire, and the fire will test what sort of work each one has done."*

You see, when our work is tested on the firing line – if it is wood, hay, and straw – it's going to burn up around us. How we build in the church – how leadership is exercised in the church (which is exactly what Paul is speaking of in this chapter) – is very, very important.

The next passage to examine is in 1 Timothy, Chapter 3. This is a chapter of the Bible with which we will become very familiar by the end of the book. Verses 14 and 15: *"I hope to come to you soon, but I am writing these things to you so that, [15] if I delay, you may know how one ought to behave in the household of God, which is the church of the living God, a pillar and buttress of truth."*

In this passage, Paul is telling Timothy why he has written him this letter, and so at the very same time God is telling you and me why he has given us this letter. So we might know how to behave ourselves in the house of God. So we might know how the church is supposed to be governed, to be led. Because that is exactly what 1 Timothy 3 is all about: qualifications for the offices of Elder and Deacon.

Let there be no mistake about this. The Bible lays down strict principles for leadership in the church, for the way in which this leadership is to be carried out. And woe be it to us if we fail to take heed of the Bible's teaching in this area. Woe be it unto us if we do not learn how to behave ourselves in the household of God.

CHAPTER 2

Historical Background

As we begin this chapter, I would like to ask a couple of hypothetical questions. I wonder how you decided which type of church government you wanted to have in the church you are attending? Assuming that most who read this book are in fact worshipping at a church with a Presbyterian form of government (are part of organizing a new one), how did you come to this decision? It seems to me that there are a number of possible reasons for such a decision. Which of these reasons is yours?

1. Perhaps being a Presbyterian is a tradition of your family. You were raised as a Presbyterian, and you have always been a Presbyterian.

2. Perhaps you are coming to this church because you just happen to like the church. You like the people, you like the pastor – whatever – and the form of church government wasn't really important to you. It happened to be Presbyterian, but that was not at all significant in your decision.

3. Perhaps you have been active in churches in the past that were governed differently but found problems in those churches which you believe stemmed from the way that they were

governed. Perhaps you were looking for a different form of church government for these reasons.

4. Perhaps you first became convinced of the truth of the Reformed faith through a newly acquired allegiance to the principles of theology known sometimes as Calvinism and then discovered that, for the most part, churches which teach this type of theology tend to be Presbyterian in church government. Perhaps you are one of these people.

5. One final possibility is that you might have decided to study what the Bible teaches about church government, and once you were able to discern that, you chose to follow that form of church government. Perhaps you were convinced Presbyterianism was the only Biblically valid form.

My guess is that you responded either to choice No. 1 (you had always been a Presbyterian) or to choice No. 2 (you like the particular church and the form of government didn't make a big difference to you). In America today, these are the two primary reasons why people begin going to any Presbyterian church.

And although I honestly believe that forms of government are crucial to the health of the church, and I believe that the Presbyterian form is the true Biblical form of church government, I want you to know that being a Presbyterian is not essential to being a Christian. You see, there are a number of doctrines or Biblical truths that are very important but that are not essential to our salvation. Certainly we must believe that Jesus is the Son of God and that he was raised from the dead. Certainly we must believe in the death of Jesus on the cross as an atonement for our sins, and that we are justified only through our faith in him and not through any merit or value or works on our own part. These are essential truths. Without such beliefs, one could not properly call himself or herself a Christian.

But there are a number of other very important truths – important doctrines – which, although clearly taught in the Bible, are not essential to our salvation. For instance, the Bible teaches clearly that it is the Word of God, that it has been inspired by God and it is true; it is all the Word of God. A very important doctrine, you would surely agree. But it is possible to be a Christian and not know this doctrine, or not fully support or understand or even believe it. Of course that would leave you in a very weak and faltering situation, but it is a possibility.

Another great truth, one that you hear from time to time around Presbyterian churches, is the doctrine of election. That God chose you before the foundations of the earth to someday profess your faith in Jesus Christ. That you were "predestined" to be a Christian. Obviously a very important and, I believe, a very true doctrine. But also one that is not essential to salvation. While surely it must make the application of Biblical truth difficult to apply in the course of evangelism as well as in the course of personal sanctification, there are people who do not believe the doctrine of election who are in fact Christians. This is another important but not "essential to salvation" doctrine.

Principles of church government fall into this same pattern. They are not essential to one's right relationship to God for salvation. One can have hope and assurance of living eternally with

Jesus in heaven and follow a form of church government that is not Presbyterian. One can be an Episcopalian, a Methodist, a Baptist, a Congregationalist, etc., and still be a Christian. I believe that during their life on this earth, throughout their efforts to apply the truths of the Kingdom of God on earth, they will have difficulties that stem from their lack of understanding of and obedience to the Scriptures in this matter. Nevertheless, principles of church government are not essential to salvation.

However, this does not mean that these principles are not important. It is important to understand that the Bible contains the inerrant word of God. It is important to understand the doctrine of election, just as it is important to follow the Biblical form of church government that we will be outlining in this book.

In the remainder of this chapter we will briefly cover some historical background on this subject. It is always helpful to understand any Biblical principle as you see how it has developed or has been followed throughout the history of the church. This review will of necessity cover only major elements of this history.

Very early in church history, most churches were governed by bishops. Each major city-church – Rome, Alexandria, Jerusalem, and so on – had its own bishop or senior clergyman. When church councils were called in those days, the bishops had to travel for many, many miles to gather. Most of the city-churches were located in the Eastern Mediterranean area, and so the bishop from the church at Rome generally arrived last. Many historians believe, that in keeping with the traditions of the day (and a Biblical principle as well), the best seat was reserved for the last arriving guest. At many of the church councils, the Bishop of Rome would sit in the presiding officer's seat, simply because he was the last to arrive.

Most of us understand a little about church history, and so we know that the role of the Bishop of Rome evolved into what we know today as the Pope of the Roman Catholic Church. Certainly, then, that denomination, as are most of the denominations with roots in this era, is governed by bishops. And this is the first of three general forms or categories of church government we will be discussing, which we will call Episcopalian. Any church that is governed by bishops in a hierarchical framework is known as an episcopacy (since the Greek word "episcopos" is frequently translated as "bishop").

This includes a number of Protestant churches as well. At the time of the Protestant Reformation, not all churches that separated from Rome changed their form of church government. Principal among these was the Church of England, or Anglican Church. As this church developed in America, it became known as the Episcopal Church, taking its name from its form of government rather than from its English heritage.

Methodists, having been a movement that grew out of the Church of England, are primarily governed as an episcopacy, although over the years they have come to put some authority into the hands of the laity. This hierarchical structure, however, still fits the Methodist Church – so much so, in fact, that for many years what we know today as the United Methodist Church was once called the Methodist Episcopal Church.

Going back to the time of the Protestant Reformation, it is very difficult to pin down Lutheranism as to its form of government. Lutherans do not insist on a uniform church polity. Some of the Lutheran denominations are Episcopal in character, and I believe that in those branches of Lutheranism that have been the least influenced by their surrounding culture, this is still the case today. Martin Luther was never originally interested in setting up a different or independent denomination or worldwide church. He merely wanted to 'reform' the Roman Catholic Church in matters of faith. Church government was never an important issue to Luther (although the absolute authority of the Pope was quite a problem to him). Luther would have been happy with bishops governing or ruling the church just so long as those bishops believed in justification by faith and the priesthood of all believers.

So you could place some Lutherans in your list of denominations governed by Episcopalian principles, and you could list some of them in the groupings of Presbyterian and Congregational as well, for in different branches of the Lutheran church, to varying degrees, all three forms of church government are found even today.

Historically speaking, the next form of government to develop was the Presbyterian form, the one we are most interested in studying in this volume. Leaders of the Protestant Reformation such as John Calvin and John Knox sought to bring about a change in the churches of their day and age to return to Biblical teaching in a number of areas, including church government. As they read their Bibles, they were convinced that government should not be placed in the hands of single individuals – of bishops – but rather in the hands of groups of men, whom they preferred to call Elders. (We will talk about these terms in much more detail later in the book.) Many of the Reformed churches growing from this age, especially the ones in Switzerland, the Netherlands, and in Scotland, practiced a form of church government known today as Presbyterian.

The third major form of church government, and one that is extremely popular in America today is known as congregationalism. Because of its great popularity throughout so many of our denominations in the United States – not just in Congregational churches, but in Baptist churches, in Bible churches, in independent churches, in charismatic and Pentecostal churches – we must have a clear understanding of the historical development of this form of government.

The central root of congregationalism can be traced back to the time of Queen Elizabeth I in England. Her goal was to enforce an absolute, rigid uniformity in all the churches in England. There were those, however, who thought differently. Puritans wanted to see the church reorganized on Presbyterian principles. Later, during the rule of Oliver Cromwell in England, they had their way for a brief period.

However, there were a few leaders who disliked the concept of a state—controlled church so much that they wanted it to be totally separate and independent. They became known in England as "Separatists" and were the forerunners of today's Congregationalists. These men contended that the church should consist only of those who had responded to the call of

Christ and who had covenanted with him and with each other to live together as his disciples.

A leading figure among the Separatists was a man named Robert Browne, who published a famous book in 1582 in which he set forth his principles of congregational church government. He claimed that churches were not subject to either ecclesiastical bishops or to secular magistrates. Ordination was not the responsibility of elders, said Browne, either alone (as bishops) or in groups (as presbyteries); but rather ordination belonged to the whole church.

As you might well understand, those people who followed Browne's line of thinking were not well received in England, and many of them had to leave the country. Some went to Holland. It was from just such a church as this, a group of English separatists living in Leyden, Holland, that the Pilgrims set off in 1620 in the Mayflower. Congregationalism became the established order in both Connecticut and Massachusetts and remained so for over two hundred years. So you can see that there is a strong historical connection between Americanism and congregationalism. In fact, the concept of the New England town meeting and democratic principles of government grows in great part from congregational church government.

The officers of a congregational church are usually a minister, a group of elders or deacons, and a church secretary and treasurer. Membership is on a profession of faith, and those who are members are then given a vote in the church meeting. All business in the church is in the hands of the congregation. They elect and call a minister; they elect elders or deacons to assist the minister in leadership. They make decisions on who should be admitted to membership and who should receive discipline. They make decisions on how and why and when to spend the funds of the church. In short, authority in the church is given to the whole congregation.

In the face of this overwhelming historical connection of congregational church government and the growth of democracy in the United States, it is very difficult indeed for people to understand that congregationalism may not in fact be what the Bible teaches, but rather is a system developed by men who were greatly oppressed by both church and civil government rulers and who wanted to exercise some freedom, both religious and civil.

And while it is our purpose in this book to show that the Presbyterian form of church government is in fact the Biblical form, we must not for one minute discount the tremendous influence that both other forms of government have had over the centuries. God has used men and churches in both congregationalism and in episcopacies to carry out the great work of his church, and probably will continue to do so in the future. And if all we had to go on was the history of the church, I'm afraid I for one would be hard pressed to come to a decision as to which form of church government to follow. (I probably would want an episcopacy if I could be a bishop!)

But our ultimate purpose is not to study church history. Our purpose is going to be to look into the Word of God, the Bible, and see if we can find there any principles of church government that God wants us to follow.

CHAPTER 3

Christl The King

Let's begin this chapter with a little high school civics lesson. We want to review the various ways in which countries – nations – have been and are being governed. Let's examine them through some caricatures. First there is the communist form of government. That's where everybody works and turns over all profits and earnings to the state, which then pays them a starvation wage and keeps all the rest of the money to spend on tanks and guns. Or something like that.

Then there is socialism. That's where everybody has his own job, but the state takes 95% of your income in taxes and turns around and gives money to everybody who asks for it for anything they need. Or something like that.

Then there is a democracy. That's where people elect other people to run their government for them and pay them a salary and expect them to perform miracles, but don't want to pay any taxes at all. Or something like that.

Then there is a monarchy, with a king (or queen). That's where the king owns everything. He is in complete control. And he sends other people around to all the cities and towns and villages and houses to be sure that the poor people are doing what they are supposed to do and paying the appropriate taxes, and the king just does whatever he wants to do, no matter whether the people like it or not. Or something like that.

While I have just given caricatures of these various forms of government, I think we all pretty much understand how they are supposed to work. We certainly detest communism, we don't like socialism, and we would rather not live under a king. No, here in America, we like good old apple pie, motherhood, and the Fourth of July democracy. That's the American way!

Don't get me wrong here. I'm not knocking democracy. I'd just as soon live under it than any other system, as long as we do what is needed to make it work and as long as we can keep corruption out of it. I'm proud that America runs on constitutional principles as a republican form of democracy. But there is a problem. And that problem is in many of the churches in America.

The problem is that because Americans are so enamored with the democratic way, they honestly believe that that is the only way to run anything, and therefore they think that is the proper way to run the Church of Jesus Christ.

If you hold this opinion, I want to say quite frankly that that is not what the Bible teaches. That is not the form of government that Jesus would have for his church, in America or in any other place in the world. The church of Jesus Christ is not to be governed simply the way we would like it, the way we think is best. The church of Jesus Christ must be governed the way the Bible tells us it is to be run. And, of course, that is the purpose of this book – to seek to determine the proper, Biblical form of church government.

The great Scottish expositor John Brown explained it this way: "A Christian Church is a very free society. But they mistake the notion who consider it a democracy. It is a monarchy, administered by inferior magistrates, chosen by their fellow subjects, who are to execute the king's law." (John Brown, *Hebrews*, Banner of Truth, 1976)

You see, what this man is saying, and saying truthfully, is that the church is a monarchy. The church of Jesus Christ is governed by a King and his magistrates.

Jesus is King of everything in the world. He is therefore the King of his church. And he is a complete and sovereign king. He's not like the king or queen of England, who hold their position in name only, and really the people run the government no matter what the king or queen says. No, Jesus is not at all that kind of puppet king or the kind of democratic monarch they have in England. He is a sovereign king. He is the supreme head of everything.

Over and over again we see this theme in the Scriptures. The prophet Zechariah gave us a famous prophesy of just this fact in Chapter 9, verse 9: *"Rejoice greatly, O daughter of Zion! Shout aloud, O daughter of Jerusalem! Behold, your king is coming to you; righteous and having salvation is he, humble and mounted on a donkey, on a colt, the foal of a donkey."* And of course the story of Jesus' triumphal entry into Jerusalem on the first Palm Sunday was clearly and inspirationally viewed by Matthew as fulfilling that great prophecy of Jesus' Kingship.

Another very famous prophetic passage of the Old Testament deals with this same theme. It is from Isaiah, Chapter 9, verses 6 and 7: *"For to us a child is born, to us a son is given; and the government shall be upon his shoulder, and his name shall be called Wonderful Counselor, Mighty God, Everlasting Father, Prince of Peace. Of the increase of his government and of peace there will be no end, on the throne of David and over his kingdom, to establish it and to uphold it with justice and with righteousness from this time forth and forevermore. The zeal of the Lord of hosts will do this."*

Of course this famous passage and its underlying story are the inspiration of so many of our great Christmas hymns, like "Angels, from the realms of glory, wing your flight o'er all the earth; Ye who sang creation's story, now proclaim Messiah's birth: Come and worship, come and worship, worship Christ, the newborn King." Or "O come, all ye faithful, joyful and triumphant, O come ye, O come ye to Bethlehem; Come and behold him born the King of angels . . ." Or "Joy to the world! the Lord is come: Let earth receive her King . . ." Throughout its history the church has always sung great hymns to this special Biblical truth: Christ is King.

However, you might be asking, "How does Christ execute his office of a King?" And that is a good question. In fact, it is one of the questions answered in the Westminster Larger Catechism, one of the historic Presbyterian confessional documents. The answer to Question 45, which we will proceed to investigate in the light of the Bible, goes as follows:

Q. How does Christ execute his office as a King?

A. Christ executes the office of a king, in calling out of the world a people to Himself, and giving them officers, laws, and censures, by which he visibly governs them, in bestowing saving grace upon his elect, rewarding their obedience, and correcting them for this sins, preserving and supporting them under all their temptations and sufferings, restraining and overcoming all their enemies, and powerfully ordering all things for his own glory, and their good, and also in taking vengeance on the rest, who know not God, and obey not the gospel.

This is a lengthy answer, but we will only deal with the portion of it that directly affects officers in the church, although we will see in fact that what the officers do is carry out just about all of these functions in the name of Christ in his church. The answer begins: "Christ executes the office of a king . . . in giving his people officers, laws, and censures, by which he visibly governs them . . ." The key words here are "officers," "laws," and "censures." Let's examine these three items in reverse order.

First, Christ gives us censures. That means that he intended for the church to discipline its people when necessary. In Matthew, Chapter 18, beginning at verse 15, Jesus tells us: "If your brother sins against you, go and tell him his fault, between you and him alone. If he listens to you, you have gained your brother. But if he does not listen, take one or two others along with you, that every charge may be established by the evidence of two or three witnesses. If he refuses to listen to them, tell it to the church. And if he refuses to listen even to the church, let him be to you as a Gentile and a tax collector. Truly, I say to you, whatever you bind on earth shall be bound in heaven, and whatever you loose on earth shall be *loosed in heaven. Again I say to you, if two of you agree on earth about anything they ask, it will be done for them by my Father in heaven. For where two or three are gathered in my name, there am I among them."*

We need to study this entire paragraph from the Bible as a unit. Too often it is separated, and it really is one paragraph – one basic concept. We often hear the last verse, *"Where two or three are gathered together in my name, there am I among of them"* quoted at a prayer meeting – especially when only a handful of people show up. And while it is true that the Lord is really with us when we enter into corporate prayer and worship, that's not what Matthew 18:20 is trying to teach us. Because this section is about church censures. It is about church discipline. In the very next verse in Matthew 18, verse 21, we find Peter asking Jesus: *"Lord, how often will my brother sin against me, and I forgive him? As many as seven times?"* Please notice, Peter wasn't talking about a prayer meeting. He was still talking about the power of the church to forgive sins – about church discipline.

You see, it was to the disciples – it was to the leaders of the church, it was to the magistrates of the King – that this power of censure was given. Christ executes his office of King in the area of censures through his magistrates. And we will be discussing church discipline at much more length and look again at that passage in Matthew in a separate chapter.

Let's now look at the second item on that list from Larger Catechism Question 45: "officers, laws, and censures." Let's look at laws. How does Christ execute the office of King by giving laws? Isaiah spelled it out pretty clearly for us in Chapter 33, verse 22: *"For the Lord is our judge; the Lord is our lawgiver; the Lord is our king; he will save us."*

Jesus is the great Lawgiver. Again, in Matthew's gospel, we find Jesus Himself picking up this theme in the Sermon on the Mount. Matthew, Chapter 5, verses 17 through 20: *"Do not think that I have come to abolish the Law or the Prophets; I have not come to abolish them but to fulfill them. For truly, I say to you, until heaven and earth pass away, not an iota, not a dot, will pass from the Law until all is accomplished. Therefore whoever relaxes one of the least of these commandments and teaches others to do the same will be called least in the kingdom of heaven, but whoever does them and teaches them will be called great in the kingdom of heaven. For I tell you, unless your righteousness exceeds that of the scribes and Pharisees, you will never enter the kingdom of heaven."*

What Jesus is teaching here is that the law applies to us. The law – the Word of God, the commandments – they are for us. That is, they are to govern our very lives, and those who do and teach these laws are the ones who will be great in the kingdom of heaven. In other words, the officers, the magistrates, those who teach and enforce the law of God in the name of the King are the leaders of the church. Christ fulfills his office of King by giving the law to his church.

Be careful that you don't read parts of the Bible which speak of the law as no longer being valid and apply that to the entire law. These are speaking only of the special civil and ceremonial laws – of the Old Testament, which foreshadowed Jesus. This "Jewish" law, as we could call it, has indeed passed away. But the law that we know today as the "Moral Law," the commandments of God – that will never pass away. Not even one 'iota' or 'dot' of the moral law has been changed.

So far we have seen the Biblical basis for the first two items on our list from Larger Catechism Question 45: "How does Christ execute the office of a King? By the giving of officers, laws, and censures." We have looked at censures. We have looked at laws. Now we must begin our look at the subject of officers. And indeed we will only begin in this chapter (for this is the heart of the entire book) to see what the Bible teaches us about officers in the church.

As we examined briefly back in Chapter One, in Paul's letter to the Ephesians, Chapter 4, the Apostle is writing about unity in the church. His main theme in the first half of this chapter is the church and how it is supposed to work together. Beginning at verse 4: *"There is one body and one Spirit—just as you were called to the one hope that belongs to your call— [5] one Lord, one faith, one baptism, [6] one God and Father of all, who is over all and through all and in all."* We see clearly Paul's theme of oneness, of unity. Now, how does this all come about? Paul continues in verse 7: *"But grace was given to each one of us according to the measure of Christ's gift."*

Recall in Chapter One we understood this key word ("apportioned" in the NIV), which was translated as a "gift" in the ESV, was speaking about something essential in the life of the church. And this apportionment – these gifts – are described beginning in verse 11: *"And he gave the apostles, the prophets, the evangelists, the pastors and teachers, [12] to equip the saints for the work of ministry, for building up the body of Christ, [13] until we all attain to the unity of the faith and of the knowledge of the Son of God, to mature manhood, to the measure of the stature of the fullness of Christ."*

We need to follow Paul's train of thought here. His goal is unity – maturity in the church. And how does this come about? Through very special, very necessary people in the church whose role is to prepare God's people for works of service. These are the special sorts of "gifts" that Christ gives to the church. And in verse 11, Paul lists four different types of officers. Remember, we need to be careful of the punctuation here. In the King James it appears that there are five items in the list, but the best way to punctuate the original Greek is to do it so there are only four items on the list: prophets, apostles, evangelists, and pastor-teachers.

And just what are these four classes of people? What are the prophets, apostles, evangelists, and pastor-teachers? Why, they are the officers by which Christ executes his office of a King. They are the magistrates through whom he rules his church.

In our next chapter, we will examine these four offices to see what they represent and which, if any, are still functioning in the church today. But for now, remember your King, Jesus Christ. And remember that this King is indeed the head of the Church. It is important that we seek to determine how our King would have us organize and function and work in the church today.

CHAPTER 4

How Many Offices Are There In The Church?

In the early days of the history of the Presbyterian Church in America – in fact, during the Second General Assembly held in Macon, Georgia in September of 1974, when the denomination was only nine months old – a question arose about whether or not Ruling Elders should be allowed to administer the Sacrament of the Lord's Supper. During the discussion on this question, it became very clear to me that the heart of the issue was not even being discussed.

Many practical points were being made on both sides of the argument, but the most decisive issue was being totally ignored. So I stepped up to a microphone and made my very first motion on the floor of a General Assembly, suggesting that the PCA appoint a study committee to look into the matter of how many offices there were in the church. Were there two, as some assumed and taught – simply Elders and Deacons? Were there three, as many others were arguing – Ministers, Elders, and Deacons? Or were there even more – including Evangelists, Teachers, etc.?

The motion to appoint the study committee passed; and lo and behold, I was one of those appointed to serve on the committee. For the next four years the PCA worked very hard on this question, actually not coming to a decision until the 6th General Assembly. It was an outgrowth of my years on this committee, coupled with some more basic work which I had done during an interim pastorate during my seminary days in which I had a great personal struggle with my own qualifications to be a Minister of the Word, that the concept of this book came into focus in my mind.

I give you this background because it is important for you to know that this is not just some academic study – something akin to how many angels can dance on the head of a pin (or if we think they ought to be dancing or not!). The issue of the number of offices in the church is vital to the health of the Presbyterian Church in America – and to any denomination for that matter. And so we want to look at some basic Biblical references to see if we can draw some conclusions to help us resolve this issue.

At the outset I must tell you that what I am presenting is the same view that I argued for on the PCA study committee, which is essentially a "two-office" position (with some variety of functions in the office of Elder). There are many godly men, in the PCA and in other Presbyterian and Reformed bodies, who hold to a "three-office" view. But since the PCA made a final decision to adopt a modified two-office view and to change its Book of Church Order accordingly, it is that view that will form the basis for this book.

Recall in the last chapter when we looked again at Ephesians, Chapter 4, verses 11 and 12, we discussed some important gifts that Jesus gave to his church in the form of leaders or officers. Verse 11 reads: *"And he gave the apostles, the prophets, the evangelists, the pastors and teachers . . ."*

Here we have a classic text of the Bible concerning offices in the church. There are four categories of them in view. Three of them are temporary offices and one is a permanent, ongoing office. Let's look at each of them.

I think we all understand the office of Apostle. They were the specially chosen disciples of Jesus who were directly called by him and who had the responsibility (and privilege) for the writing of the New Testament scriptures. And we all understand, I believe, that this office has ceased – that when the Apostles died, their special gifts and function, as well as their office, died with them. We do not have any more Apostles today. We do not have any more Scripture being written today. The canon is closed. The Book is finished.

The same holds true for the office of Prophet. Now, there certainly were people in both the Old and New Testament ages who were gifted with prophesy, and could be called "prophets" with a small "p." But that is not what Paul has in view in this verse. Rather, he is speaking about Prophets with a capital "P." He is speaking about men who were used in special leadership offices by God, particularly in the responsibility for authorship of the Old Testament scriptures.

So, what is in view here is not only the four major and twelve minor Prophets whose names many memorized as children in Sunday school. Also in view are the authors of the historical books (sometimes referred to as the "former prophets") and Moses as the author of the first five books of the Old Testament – in fact, to each and every author of the Old Testament scriptures. These were indeed special leaders – gifts that Christ gave to the church. But those leaders are no longer with us today. The office of Prophet has passed from the scene.

I believe that this same logic can be applied to the next office that Paul mentions in Ephesians 4:11, the office of Evangelist. While it is true that there are people yet today who do the function of evangelism (even some doing it "full time"), and that evangelism is something in and of itself that is of ongoing importance in the church, the special New Testament office of Evangelist is something different.

This was the special office of "apostolic helper," such as Timothy and Titus fulfilled – an office that had along with it some special gifts, miraculous gifts if you will (as did Apostles and Prophets). And this special, temporary office has passed from the scene. We no longer have the New Testament office of Evangelist active in the church today.

But I want now to move on to the one permanent, continuing office the Paul includes on his list in Ephesians 4:11 – the office of "Pastor-Teacher." As I mentioned in the previous chapter, we need to be careful about punctuation in the English translation of this verse. Most modern translations have got the emphasis correct. The best way to view this term is as a hyphenated word, "Pastor-Teacher," or as the ESV does by connecting them with a separate article, and not as two separate terms or offices.

The Pastor-Teacher of Ephesians 4:11 is the one ongoing, continuing permanent office in the church today from that verse. And where do we find that office? Where do we find it in the visible church and, even more importantly, where do we find it in the rest of the New Testament? Well, the answer comes in our understanding the office of Elder. You see, the terms "Elder," "Bishop" ("Overseer") and "Pastor-Teacher" all refer to one and the same office.

The first thing we need to understand about this principle is that in no verse of Scripture are the terms Elder and Bishop (Overseer) and Pastor-Teacher used to refer to two (or more) different groups or classes of people. Nowhere can you find any of the New Testament writers speaking about these offices in any way referring to them as two or three different groups.

While this is an argument from silence, it is an important argument. For in all the many greetings given in the New Testament epistles, it would be very surprising to find that these terms were not used separately for different groups if in fact there were such separate groups in existence in the churches of the time.

Let's begin with Philippians 1:1: *"Paul and Timothy, servants of Christ Jesus, to all the saints in Christ Jesus who are at Philippi, with the overseers and deacons . . ."* Here we have Paul writing a letter to the church located at Philippi, and in his greetings he singles out the leaders – the officers. And he calls them "Overseers" and "Deacons." Now, in some translations the term "Overseers" is translated as 'Bishops.' And indeed these two English words are used to describe the same office, as they are both proper translations of the same Greek word.

The Greek word in view is "episcopos," and the root of that word involves oversight. It is from this word that the Episcopalian form of government gets its name, specifying that the church should be ruled by "episcapoi" or 'Bishops.' I believe that Philippians 1:1 is a classic text. It speaks very clearly to the issue that there were two offices in the church at Philippi – Bishops and Deacons.

Let's look at another of the New Testament churches, the church located at Ephesus – the same church to which Paul had addressed his letter which contained that verse (4:11) that we have spent so much time on, the verse that spoke of the office of "Pastor-Teacher." Are there any other offices in the church at Ephesus? We find our answer in Acts, Chapter 20.

In this chapter, beginning at verse 13, we find Paul (along with Luke, the author of Acts) traveling to Jerusalem from Macedonia. Paul was in a hurry to get to Jerusalem. In fact, verse 16 tells us he decided not to visit the church in Ephesus, and he had landed on the Asia Minor coast at Miletus.

But Paul wanted to speak to the leaders of the church from Ephesus. So he sent for them, and they met him at Miletus. In verses 18 through 35, we have an extremely moving, emotional scene as Paul addresses them and gives them his final blessings and words of encouragement, knowing that he would probably never see these men, who were so beloved to him, again.

Given this very important meeting with the leadership of the church in Ephesus, the same church to which Paul had written speaking of "Pastor-Teachers" as gifts being given to them, who are the leaders that Paul sends for to come to Miletus? In verse 17 it is very clear. He sends for the *"Elders."* The Greek word in view is "presbuteros," from which we get our English words presbyter and Presbyterian.

Just who are these Elders? Are they some new, some different group of leaders about which we know nothing else? Verse 28 contains our answer. Paul says to these Elders: *"Pay careful attention to yourselves and to all the flock, in which the Holy Spirit has made you overseers, to care for the church of God, which he obtained with his own blood."*

The word "Overseer" here is exactly that same word we saw in Philippians 1:1, the Greek word "episcopos." You see, in Paul's mind the word "Elder" is synonymous with the word "Bishop" or "Overseer." They are not something different. They are in fact two different titles for the same New Testament office.

Notice also that he refers to them as Shepherds. Now the word "shepherd" comes from the same Greek root word that the word "pastor" comes from. A "Pastor" is a "Shepherd." A Shepherd is a Pastor. And so the very same group of men are called three different things in this passage: "Elders," "Bishops (or Overseers)," and "Pastors (or Shepherds)." Three different titles for one and the same office.

If we turn to Titus, Chapter 1, we find Paul writing to one of his special "apostolic helpers" who is working with the church in Crete, yet another of the New Testament churches. And who are the leaders of the church in Crete? Well, as you read

Chapter 1 of Titus, beginning at verse 5, it is quite clear that the Elders are the leaders: *"This is why I left you in Crete* [Paul writes to Titus], *so that you might put what remained into order, and appoint elders in every town as I directed you—"*

And then he goes on to discuss qualifications for this leadership office. Verse 6: *"if anyone* {antecedent obviously any Elder) *is above reproach, the husband of one wife, and his children are believers and not open to the charge of debauchery or insubordination."*

Now, notice carefully what Paul does as he continues in verse 7: *"For an overseer, as God's steward, must be above reproach. he must not be arrogant or quick-tempered or a drunkard or violent or greedy for gain . . ."* And then he continues on with more qualifications.

You see, Paul does it again! He refers to these same groups of leaders by different terms. This time he calls them both Elders and Overseers (or Bishops) in the same context, almost in the same breath. Once again we see one office of leadership in the church, but with different names – Elder and Bishop.

Notice also in verse 9 that one of the very important qualifications for this leader is the ability to teach. This same idea is repeated in 1 Timothy 3, and we will look at that in great detail later on in the book. My point here is that the title of "Pastor-Teacher" is quite in keeping with the role of an Elder/Bishop.

I believe the New Testament evidence is overwhelming. There is a single office of leadership in the church of Jesus that carries a number of titles. In different places and for different reasons, this one office is sometimes called "Elder," sometimes called

"Bishop" or "Overseer," and is sometimes called "Pastor-Teacher." These are not different offices; they are all the same office, with different titles.

It is also important to see that this interpretation is in keeping with the understanding the people of God had since Old Testament days. There is a sense of continuity of government within the church in both the Old and New Testaments. The Old Testament and the Gospels provide crucial background information to the church government erected by the Apostles.

In Exodus 3:16, when sent by God to deliver the Israelites from Egyptian bondage, Moses was told to *"gather the elders of Israel together."* So from these very early days we have Old Testament evidence of the rule of the people of God by Elders.

Also during the time of Moses, Elders are shown in a number of passages (Deuteronomy 21:19, Exodus 24:12, Numbers 11:16, Leviticus 4:15) to be both rulers and covenantal representatives of the people.

Elders are seen in the time of the Judges, the period of the Kings, and the time of Babylonian captivity.

Elders provide leadership in rebuilding the temple after the return from exile. Information on Jewish history during the intertestamental period also bears witness to the rule of Elders in the synagogues.

At the time of Christ's advent, references are found to the "Elders," "Rulers," and "Rulers of the synagogue." Although

Jewish leadership was quite corrupt at this time, it is important to note that the Jews had not become so apostate as to allow the Biblical office of Elder to fall totally into disuse.

The primary point to be made here is that the Apostles of the New Testament did not create something radically new. They built on the foundation of previous Biblical revelation. When the apostles addressed their readers concerning church officers, the readers had in mind much of the governmental framework that they found in the Old Testament. Therefore, a Presbyterian rule (that is to say, rule by Elders) is not simply New Testament church government; it is in fact Biblical church government.

One final point we need to make in this chapter about the office of Elder concerns the absolute necessity for a plurality of Elders in each church. In no case do you find a New Testament church that is governed by only one Elder or Bishop. The Jerusalem church included "Apostles and Elders" (Acts 11:1, 15:2). The church in Antioch has "Prophets and Teachers," both in the plural (Acts 13:1). We've already examined Ephesus, Philippi and Crete, all of which had "Elders" or "Bishops" in the plural.

This plurality of Elders follows logically from the clear fact that only Jesus is the head of the church. Paul teaches this truth explicitly in two of his letters, Ephesians (1:20-23, 5:23) and Colossians (1:18). And since there can clearly be only one king (one "senior leader" if you will) in each church, it should follow that there must be a plurality of his "under-shepherds" or mag-istrates in each church.

We need to be careful to understand that even the existence of Apostles in the New Testament does not imply the need for "Bishops" to be in charge of a church or group of churches today. The Apostles, recall, were only a temporary, special office. It is not a continuing office in the church today.

Even in their own day and age, when the Apostles exercised church government in the New Testament, they acted as Elders. In Acts 15, which we will examine more thoroughly later in the book, they act with other Elders. In Galatians 2, Acts 12, and again in Acts 15, we see the Apostles subject to one another and to the Elders of the church. When acts of ordination were carried out in the church (another subject to be taken up in more detail later), the Apostles do not act unilaterally, but rather they function along with other Elders (Acts 6:6, 1 Tim 4:14, 2 Tim 1:6).

At least two of the Apostles, John and Peter, call themselves Elders in their own letters. Clearly these Apostles understood they had two separate functions: the Apostolate and their role of leadership in the church as Elders.

So we have seen that in the New Testament church there are today no more than two continuing offices – the one of oversight and leadership which is known by the different titles of Elder, Bishop, and/or Pastor-Teacher. And the office of Deacon, which will be discussed separately. In the next chapter we will look at the function of Elders, and to point out the specifics that make those men who are known as Ministers of the Word today differ-ent in function from those known commonly as Ruling Elders.

But even in pointing out these differences, we want to set the basic stage with the point that they're all in the same office – the key leadership and oversight office of the Bible known as Elder.

CHAPTER 5

The Function of Elders

Before discussing the function of Elders, let me first explain why I have chosen to use the term 'Elder' as the primary title for this office. Recall we saw the writers of Scripture referring to this leadership office sometimes by the title of Elder, sometimes by the title of Bishop (or Overseer), and sometimes by the title of Pastor-Teacher. Why chose Elder as the primary title? Of course it has long been the tradition of church history, at least in that branch of church history concerning Presbyterianism. No sense changing tradition if it is not needed. But there are other good reasons as well.

One is that this usage is in keeping with the background of the very word Elder. The word has a strong Jewish origin. The people of God in the Old Testament understood what Elders were all about. There was an emphasis in this word on the issues of maturity and wisdom and dignity. And I believe these are proper emphases to carry over even today.

The word Bishop or Overseer has a more Greek origin, and in this word the emphasis is more on function than on personal qualities. The principal function in view is that of ruling, of being in charge. While that may be a suitable emphasis for an Episcopalian form of government, where the term Bishop is commonly used, as we learn more and more about these leaders in the church we will see that the better emphasis to make – and therefore the better title to use for this office – is in fact Elder.

It would be difficult to use the term Pastor, or Pastor-Teacher for this office today, because of the common understanding in our culture that these terms only apply to ordained clergymen, to Ministers of the Word. A little later we will see some functional differences that make ordination important and that set aside certain Elders for particular service in the church. But the one thing that all these church leaders have in common is what we want to stress at this point; and to this end, the word Elder must be our choice.

Turning now to the issue of function, if you had to come up with just one, central, universal concept or term or idea that best describes what it is that Elders do in the church of Jesus Christ, I believe that term would be oversight. Let's see that truth in a couple of portions of the New Testament. First, let's look at 1 Peter, Chapter 5, verses 1 and 2. Peter writes: *"So I exhort the elders among you, as a fellow elder and a witness of the sufferings of Christ, as well as a partaker in the glory that is going to be revealed: [2] shepherd the flock of God that is among you, exercising oversight, not under compulsion, but willingly, as God would have you; not for shameful gain, but eagerly;"*

I think you will agree that these two verses are giving us the proper context. Peter (remember, he is an Apostle) is calling himself an Elder. He understood his dual role, and at this point he is stressing the role of Elder. In fact, he is addressing other

Elders. And what does he tell them? He tells them to be good shepherds, good pastors. And what is the key thing that they need to know and to do in order to be good shepherds, to be Biblical Elders? They must serve as Overseers. That, says Peter, is the key to the office of Elder – oversight.

In Hebrews, Chapter 13, verse 17, while the term Overseer is not used, the same idea is very clear. It reads: *"Obey your leaders and submit to them, for they are keeping watch over your souls, as those who will have to give an account. Let them do this with joy and not with groaning, for that would be of no advantage to you."* The issues, I believe, are very clear. Obedience. Submission. Leadership. Authority. Watching over. All of these add up to serving as Overseers. We will be looking at this verse in Hebrews, as well as the verses in 1 Peter, again as we examine the detailed functions of Elders more closely. But keep in mind as we go through this chapter that the one key issue, the most important idea or theme concerning Elders in the church, is wrapped up in the word oversight.

Now, just what is it that Elders are supposed to do? What are the specific functions they are to carry out as overseers in the church of Jesus Christ today? Pastor Al Martin, a Reformed Baptist minister in New Jersey, uses three very helpful Biblical illustrations in his preaching to describe the functions of Elders in the church. Martin (to whom I am deeply indebted for the ideas in this chapter) says there appear to be in the Scriptures three different, important functions that Elders carry out. Elders function in the same way as: (1) fathers in a family, (2) shepherds in a flock, and (3) rulers in an assembly. Let's look at these three illustrations to learn about the functions of elders.

How is it that an Elder functions as a Father in his family? Well, we can look to 1 Timothy 3, verses 4 and 5. Recall this is going to be a very important chapter to us before we finish this series. In this passage Paul is listing the qualifications for Elders: "*He must manage his own household well, with all dignity keeping his children submissive, [5] for if someone does not know how to manage his own household, how will he care for God's church?*" Paul's illustration is quite simple. He says if a man can't be a Biblical father, then he certainly can't be a Biblical Elder.

Paul makes the same analogy, only in reverse order, in Ephesians 5:22-24. In this classic passage dealing with marriage and family relationships, Paul writes: "*Wives, submit to your own husbands, as to the Lord. [23] For the husband is the head of the wife even as Christ is the head of the church, his body, and is himself its Savior. [24] Now as the church submits to Christ, so also wives should submit in everything to their husbands.*" You see, the analogy is very strong between leadership and authority in the church, and in the family. So it is helpful for us to view the role of Elders in the church in relationship to that of fathers in a family.

And what is it that fathers do? What is the function of a father in a family? Well, fathers provide food and shelter. They are responsible for the financial needs of the family. They are a source of safety and well-being, of protection. They are responsible for education and discipline. In carrying out their duties, they frequently delegate some authority to their wives. And all of these are things that have very close analogy in the church, as we will see specifically in just a few moments.

The second illustration that will help us understand Elders is that of shepherds. Let's see now how Elders function as shepherds in a flock. Looking once again at 1 Peter 5:2: "*Shepherd the flock of God that is among you, exercising oversight . . .*" You see, in addressing the Elders of the church, Peter tells them to be good shepherds, to care for their flocks. While not all Elders during New Testament times had been shepherds (Peter himself had been a commercial fisherman), they would have been familiar with the function of shepherds. Especially Peter, who learned this lesson the hard way.

Recall the scene recounted for us by the Apostle John in his Gospel, Chapter 21, beginning at verse 15. The setting for the scene is after the Resurrection, after Jesus had begun to make his appearance known to his followers, to demonstrate to them that he was indeed alive and that he had been raised from the dead. John tells us of the very special conversation he had with Peter: "*When they had finished breakfast, Jesus said to Simon Peter, "Simon, son of John, do you love me more than these?" he said to him, "Yes, Lord; you know that I love you." he said to him, "Feed my lambs." [16] he said to him a second time, "Simon, son of John, do you love me?" he said to him, "Yes, Lord; you know that I love you." he said to him, "Tend my sheep." [17] he said to him the third time, "Simon, son of John, do you love me?" Peter was grieved because he said to him the third time, "Do you love me?" and he said to him, "Lord, you know everything; you know that I love you." Jesus said to him, "Feed my sheep."*

In the context of restoring Peter into full fellowship as a follower, as a disciple (indeed, as an Elder), Jesus spoke to him in terms of shepherding, in terms of sheep. And why did he do this?

Because Jesus Himself is the Good Shepherd. Jesus had modeled this function Himself, and Peter would have clearly understood exactly what Jesus had in mind. And so now, writing to other Elders in the church, Peter can, with the authority that comes from personal experience, tell them to be good shepherds.

And just what is a good shepherd? What is it that shepherds do? While not many Americans today have any direct familiarity with the function of shepherds, most Christians at least are familiar with the Twenty-Third Psalm. That passage tells us a lot about the function of shepherds. You may want to open your Bibles to read over the Psalm. And as you do, look at few of the action verbs that are used by David in speaking about the Lord being his shepherd. *"He makes me lie down." "He restores." "He leads." "His rod and staff comfort."* The shepherd is *"with"* his sheep. The shepherd *"feeds"* his sheep. Certainly the loving care that a good shepherd provides for his flock is exactly that analogy that Peter had in mind that Elders were to carry out in relationship to their 'flock,' the church.

There is a third Biblical illustration that helps us understand the function of Elders in the church, and this is the illustration of a ruler in an assembly. ('Assembly' could refer to a King's court, to a parliament, to the U. S. Congress – or even to a state legislature or town council.) Let's see now how it is that an Elder functions in that capacity.

In Hebrews 13 the author is making some concluding remarks to the Christians to whom he is writing, especially in the area of interpersonal relationships. He starts with marriage, and then switches in verse 7 to the topic of church leadership: *"Remember your leaders, those who spoke to you the word of God. Consider the outcome of their way of life, and imitate their faith."* Certainly the leaders in view here are church leaders, not secular government leaders. These are leaders who have faith in Jesus – leaders who speak the Word of God. In other words, these are Elders.

Looking now at verse 17: "Obey your leaders and submit to them, for they are keeping watch over your souls, as those who will have to give an account. Let them do this with joy and not with groaning, for that would be of no advantage to you." What is being discussed here is the role of a ruler in an assembly. The author speaks in terms of obedience and submission, of keeping watch, of giving an account. These are clearly terms of ruling-style leadership.

You find the same thing in 1 Thessalonians 5:12-13: *"We ask you, brothers, to respect those who labor among you and are over you in the Lord and admonish you, [13] and to esteem them very highly in love because of their work. Be at peace among yourselves."* Here are the same issues again. Someone is "over" someone else, in a position of rule. They even admonish those under them. Again, the illustration of a ruler.

"Ruler" could refer to men in many different leadership roles. I spent 22 years on active duty in the United States Navy, so when I think of a ruler, I think of a Division Officer, the leader most directly in charge of a group of men (and women) in the service, something like a Company Commander or a Platoon Leader in the Army or Marines. Someone who has leadership, has "ruling" functions, but who is also responsible higher up the chain of command to an ultimate commanding officer. Not someone with absolute power and authority, but rather someone with delegated authority, but with enough of that authority to carry out his responsibilities.

Division Officers don't just tell people what to do. They are responsible to see that the needs of their people are met as well. They have to worry about where their people live and eat, whether they are qualified to carry out their assignments, whether they are ready for advancement to the next position of responsibility – in other words, caring for their total military life.

Rulers (at least Biblical rulers) are not just little dictators. They are responsible leaders who really have caring for people as their primary function. This, then, is the third illustration that helps us to understand what the functions of Elders in the church are today. Elders are fathers, are shepherds, and are rulers.

Before we turn to specific tasks for which Elders are responsible, we want to go back to that issue which concerns how Ministers of the Word fit into the broader category of Elders. There is one key verse on this issue in the Bible, and we want to look at that verse and then make some logical applications. In 1 Timothy 5, Paul is continuing with instructions to Timothy concerning the role of a number of different people in the church. At verse 17 he gets to a special case concerning Elders. He writes: *"Let the elders who rule well be considered worthy of double honor, especially those who labor in preaching and teaching."*

It appears that Paul's main object in this section is to point out that some Elders receive payment, receive wages for the work they do in the church. Perhaps some were reluctant to pay them enough, and Paul is making it very clear that their tasks are worthy of payment. In fact, he calls it *"double honor."* And who are these Elders who receive payment for carrying out their tasks? Certainly not every Elder; only some are singled out. And Paul says two things about them. They *"rule well"* and they *"labor in preaching and teaching."*

This means that there is a group of Elders who work in preaching and teaching. They find their employment in these tasks. Throughout the history of churches since the Reformation, especially those in the family known as Presbyterian, these are the men who have been most commonly called Teaching Elders or Ministers of the Word. The church over the centuries has developed a very important tradition that there be a trained clergy who carry out special tasks in the church, especially preaching and administration of the sacraments, and that they be paid for conducting these tasks. Not that some Ruling Elders cannot be employed if they, as Paul says, *"direct the affairs of the church well."* And so there are some Ruling Elders who are employees of the church at the local, Presbytery, and denominational level as well.

The important point here is the Elder who *"labors in preaching and teaching."* Notice that this is not a special office. There are not three types of offices in the church – Deacons, Elders, and Ministers. Ministers of the Word are simply Elders, equal in responsibility and authority, but with some specialized functions and tasks for which they are paid. Later we will discuss how some of the specific tasks are best divided up between Teaching and Ruling Elders. But for now let's be sure we understand that all Elders – Teaching and Ruling – all have the same basic functions. They all serve together, following the model of being a father, a shepherd, and a ruler, as they carry out the work of leadership in the church of Jesus Christ.

CHAPTER 6

The Tasks of Elders

In the past two chapters we have looked closely at the office of Elder, finding from the Scriptures its origin, its uniqueness, and some very helpful descriptions of the functions of the office. In this chapter we want to become a little more specific about what it is that Elders actually do in the church of Jesus Christ. And so we will turn our attention from basic principles and functions to some specific tasks.

I believe most people understand the difference between a function and a task. For instance, being a carpenter is a function. But some of the tasks involved are being able to hammer a nail straight (which I have never been able to do), being able to saw a straight cut in a board (another impossible task!) and other such tasks that carpenters need to do to carry out their function.

Or how about a banker? He needs to be able to handle many tasks involving the use and care of money. Or a soldier? He has many specific tasks for which he spends weeks and months in training to learn so he can fulfill his function.

The same thing can be said of Elders. They have a number of tasks that are important to their exercising leadership in the church. To begin with, we can find two summary tasks under which nearly everything else they do will ultimately fall. And to find those two summary tasks, we want to look at a key chapter for our study in this book – 1 Timothy 3. At verse 14, Paul is writing to his young helper: "*I hope to come to you soon, but I am writing these things to you so that, [15] if I delay, you may know how one ought to behave in the household of God . . .*"

It is quite clear that Paul has written this chapter – this entire letter, for that matter – to give instructions in church government. And so it is understandable that the instructions contained in Chapter 3 concerning Elders and Deacons are forming such an important part of our study in this book.

In verse 2, Paul writes concerning Elders: "*Therefore an overseer must be above reproach, the husband of one wife, sober-minded, self-controlled, respectable, hospitable, able to teach . . .*" Then he goes on with more qualifications for the office. Notice that right in the middle of this list of subjective qualifications, most of which concern the man's personality and ability to deal with other people, we find this more objective requirement: the Elder must be able to teach.

This task of teaching is vital to the function of every Elder. Without this ability to pass on the truth of the Scriptures to other people, the Elder cannot really function in his office. Now, what does this task of teaching involve? Does Paul mean that every Elder must have professional training as a teacher? I don't think so. Paul himself gives a very good commentary on this task in a parallel chapter of the Bible. In Titus, Chapter 1, Paul is writing to his other key assistant concerning exactly the same thing he discusses with Timothy. Verse 5: "*This is why I left you in Crete, so*

*that you might put what remained into order, and appoint elders in
every town as I directed you."*

You see, Titus, Chapter 1, is also about organizing church
government and contains another list of qualifications for men
who are to function in that office. Looking down in that list of
qualifications to verse 9 we find: *"He must hold firm to the
trustworthy word as taught, so that he may be able to give
instruction in sound doctrine and also to rebuke those who
contradict it."*

I believe Titus 1:9 is the very best commentary on what Paul
means when he says an Elder must be able to teach. He means
that every Elder must be able to use the *"sound doctrine"* of the
Bible, the truth of God's Word that he has been taught, and use
this truth to do two basic things: *"give instruction"* and *"rebuke
those who contradict it."* This is the essence of the teaching task
of Elders. It might be standing before an audience of many thousands preaching the Word. It might mean teaching a large adult
Sunday school class or a small nursery-age class. It might mean
leading a small group Bible study. It might mean speaking one-
on-one with someone in the church or a neighbor or a work
associate. The number of people involved is not important. The
style, the format, is not important.

What is important is that every Elder must be able to carry out
the task of using the Word of God to encourage other Christians
and to refute the opposition of non-Christians (sometimes even
to refute their opposition to the end that they themselves
become believers; we call that evangelism). This then is the first
of our two primary tasks of an Elder: teaching.

Looking back to our key chapter, 1 Timothy 3, we will see the other primary task: ruling. Verses 4 and 5: *"He* (the Elder) *must manage his own household well, with all dignity keeping his children submissive, [5] for if someone does not know how to manage his own household, how will he care for God's church?"*

Here in 1 Timothy the ruling is put into the context of a family illustration. In 1 Peter 5 it was the illustration of being a shepherd of a flock. In Hebrews we saw the task put in the context of the church itself, which is also true of 1 Thessalonians, Chapter 5. So no matter what the illustration used, the same truth applies. Every Elder is responsible for some element of ruling, of exercising authority. So there are two primary tasks for every Elder: the task of ruling and the task of teaching.

In our Presbyterian traditions of the 21st century, especially in my denomination (PCA), we have the habit of referring to the two different types of Elders in terms of these two tasks. We call Ministers of the Word 'Teaching Elders,' and we call the men elected from within the local congregation 'Ruling Elders.' In some ways these are helpful references, for certainly the Minister of the Word is seen more in the role of teaching and the locally-elected Elder is seen more in the role of ruling. But that does not mean that these two tasks are somehow separated. All Elders must fulfill the task of ruling. And so the Minister of the Word is to be an active participant in the decision-making process of the church. And all Elders must fulfill the task of teaching and not just leave it all to the paid professionals.

In the next chapter we will be talking more about how these tasks are carried out in the church today. We will be talking about issues involving power and authority. But for the rest of this chapter I want to zero in on a few more specifics of the general tasks of teaching and ruling.

We have already looked at Titus 1:9, which tells us that Elders must be able to exhort, to encourage, and to convince or refute. But as he continues in Chapter 1 of the letter to Titus, Paul gives us some application of this task. He tells Titus that there are some rebellious people in the church at Crete who are teaching falsehoods, who are in fact trying to spread heresy. One task of the Elder, then, is to keep out this heresy.

This was the same thing Paul told the Ephesians Elders in that scene described for us in Acts, Chapter 20. There in that meeting at Miletus, Paul told them, in verses 29 through 31: "*I know that after my departure fierce wolves will come in among you, not sparing the flock; [30] and from among your own selves will arise men speaking twisted things, to draw away the disciples after them. [31] Therefore be alert . . .*"

Paul wanted these Elders to be ready to carry out this very important task in the church of Jesus Christ – the protecting of the truth, the guarding against heresy. Every Elder is charged with that responsibility and needs to hear that warning from Paul, even today – especially today – when there are so many heresies, so many errors abounding in the church.

This passage in Acts 20 gives us another important task for Elders to carry out as well. It is in verse 28, which we examined earlier. The illustration of being good shepherds – which includes that most important task of shepherds, feeding of the flock. If shepherds were responsible for the guarding, the safe-keeping of their flock, they were just as importantly responsible for their feeding. Recall this was the injunction that Jesus gave to Peter: *"Feed my lambs. Feed my flock."* And that same injunction stands yet today for every Elder. They must fulfill the task of feeding the flock of God, the people in the church. And so preaching and teaching – the whole gamut of education tasks – are the responsibility of all the Elders.

Before we leave this passage in Acts 20, let's see one more task that is the responsibility of Elders. Verse 35: *"In all things I have shown you that by working hard in this way we must help the weak and remember the words of the Lord Jesus, how he himself said, 'It is more blessed to give than to receive.'"* You see, Elders have the responsibility to care for the needy, the poor, the weak. We will be seeing a bit later in the book that this task can be delegated to the other continuing office in the church – to Deacons. But let us never forget that this task is an essential responsibility of the Elders.

What other specific tasks can we think of that Elders must do? Remember that verse we read earlier in another context in 1 Thessalonians 5:12? There Paul said, *"We ask you, brothers, to respect those who labor among you and are over you in the Lord and admonish you."* One of the necessary tasks of Elders is to admonish others in the church. This task, which is very much a combination of the teaching and ruling functions, involves the matter of exercising church discipline. This particular task is so important we will be spending an entire chapter on it a bit later. But this task is the responsibility of the Elders, all of them functioning together.

Another verse we looked at earlier was Hebrews 13:7. Recall it said: *"Remember your leaders, those who spoke to you the word of God. Consider the outcome of their way of life, and imitate their faith."* This verse gives us several additional tasks. *"Speaking the Word of God"* is the first. Elders must be able to speak the Word of God, and so the clear implication is that they had better know what it says. Elders, both Ruling Elders and Teaching Elders, must be well versed in the contents of the Bible. And they must be able to *"speak"* that Word to others.

Another task involves living a life of faith. In a sense this is a subjective quality, and we will look at it in much more detail in the chapter on qualifications for church office. But in an objective way, the task of every Elder is to live that life of faith – to go about one's business each day showing that he is able to apply the truths of Scripture to every aspect of his calling, of his responsibility – not just in the church, but in his family, in his vocation, in his neighborhood, in whatever sphere of life God has called him to serve.

One other very important task of the Elders of the church involves prayer. We see this in the Epistle of James, Chapter 5. Beginning at verse 13, James admonishes Christians concerning the issue of prayer. And in verse 14, he says: *"Is anyone among you sick? Let him call for the elders of the church, and let them pray over him, anointing him with oil in the name of the Lord."*

Clearly the Elders have the task to pray for those in the church that have special needs, going so far as to symbolize the Spirit of God by anointing the sick. This task of prayer is vital to the health of every church. Any Session (Board of Elders) that goes about their duties in a purely businesslike way without sincerely, honestly bathing every decision they make – every person in the church who has a need – with prayer will be a Session that fails in its responsibilities. Elders must carry out this important task of prayer consistently and regularly.

We could probably go on and on with illustrations of specific tasks for which Elders are held responsible, but let's shift gears a little bit now. Let's see some of the practical implications that these specific tasks spelled out for us in the Bible take in the particular church today. What goes on in our churches that the Elders need to be involved in and look after?

How about preaching? Whose responsibility is preaching in the church? I know a number of people who say that only the preacher, only the Minister of the Word has that responsibility. But I believe that idea stems from a three-office view, from understanding Ministers of the Word as something basically different from Ruling Elders. But if in fact all Elders are in the same office, then the Elders together have the responsibility for preaching. While it should be only the ordained and installed Teaching Elders who regularly carry out the actual task of writing and delivering sermons, it is certainly the task of all the Elders together to decide what ought to be preached. What are the current needs of the people in the church? Is there a particular subject or a particular book of Scripture that would be more relevant and more important than another? These decisions belong to all the Elders.

How about the worship service? And the music ministry? Do you simply appoint or hire an organist and/or choir director and let them make all the decisions concerning music? Maybe none of the Elders are gifted musically. Well, we must be very careful here. The entire content of a worship service, including the preaching, the prayers, the readings, the music – all of this – is vital to the health of the people of God. None of this can be delegated to others by the Elders without careful control. Ultimately the Elders have responsibility, and they should therefore exercise authority. Not every hymn ever written is suitable for singing in a worship service. Not every possible item of an order of worship is appropriate for use on Sunday morning. Judgment and care must be exercised in these matters, and the responsibility must finally rest with the Elders.

The same thing can be said for the administration of the sacraments. I believe it is vitally important that only Elders be involved in the administration of the sacraments. Certainly a Teaching Elder must lead in the service. This is a visible form of the Word, always to be connected to preaching. Using anyone else other than Elders, even in the distribution of the elements of the Lord's Supper, presents a picture that says that we don't take this part of the church's ministry too seriously. We don't have to see who takes the elements at communion. It in fact gives the impression that discipline is not being exercised. We will discuss the issue of discipline at more length in a later chapter, but my point here is that this is the responsibility of the Elders, and they must exercise this responsibility with great care.

The Christian Education program falls in the same category. You can't turn C. E. over to a non-Elder and just let it go. Whether that person is a trained Director of Christian Education from a college or just someone from the congregation who has

a lot of experience in teaching Sunday school, the total education program of the church must remain under the control of
the Elders. Approval of curriculum. Training and examination of
teachers. Supplying of proper equipment and space. All of these
items fall under the tasks of Elders.

This does not mean, of course, that there cannot be committees or ministry teams appointed in the church to give advice
and recommendations and to help with the routine operation of
the various ministries. But it is important that they be just that –
committees, not self-standing boards. Giving advice and recommendations, not making policy decisions. These are such important tasks that the Elders dare not delegate them so far away that
they lose touch with them.

I would strongly encourage any church – whether it is a mission church just organizing and about to have Elders for the very
first time, or whether it is a 200-year-old church with a long history of "we've always done it that way" – to make a careful
examination of the role of Elders in the church. What are the
tasks that others in the church are doing? Are those tasks properly under the authority and jurisdiction of the Elders? Can
someone else make decisions on how and why and when to
spend money? Can Deacons (or Trustees) be given control of the
financial aspects of a church's ministry and the Elders of the
church still be able to give an account to God for their tasks and
functions in the church? These are difficult questions, of course,
but my point is that if Elders function as fathers, as shepherds,
and as rulers – that if their tasks involve all teaching and ruling
in the church – then every task that is carried out in the church
must ultimately come under their responsibility and authority.

CHAPTER 7

Power and Authority

In the last several chapters we have been talking about the exercise of leadership in the church as exercised by the office of Elder. In this chapter we want to examine the question of how that leadership is exercised, and leave the issue of who exercises it settled and behind us.

In an earlier chapter I mentioned the fact that in each of the earliest developing New Testament churches, there was clearly a plurality of Elders in leadership. In other words, the church was not to be governed by the decision making of only one person, such as a bishop or pope. Rather, it was to be governed by groups of Elders working together.

This is one of the most important points in the Biblical form of church government, but it is one that is frequently misunderstood, wrongly practiced, and maligned in today's churches, even in many Presbyterian churches. And yet an understanding of the dynamics should help us understand how important this issue really is.

Many churches in this country are run by one powerful leader, normally the senior pastor. In the episcopacies, particularly in the Roman Catholic Church, this is done by design. But in many other forms of church government, even Presbyterian and congregational, the same thing is true. This one strong leader becomes what we might call a "religious dictator." Not that he has any intention or motivation to function or act this way. It is merely his particular style of leadership, and probably not even a style he studied or learned – just one that came naturally to him through his background and experience.

Having a single leader has a number of sociological and theological problems attached to it, apart from its not being the basic form of church government taught in the Scriptures. First of all, there is the clear problem with sin. No one is free of sin, and whatever the area of weakness or temptation or sin might be in the life of this one particular leader, you can be sure that Satan will mount his attack against that church at just that point. For surely that presents to the enemy a clear opening.

Even if one could find a leader without any problem areas (which I doubt is possible, practically speaking, let alone a valid theological point), there is also the issue of the overwhelming amount of responsibility and work that then falls on this leader's shoulders. In even a small-to-medium sized congregation, the responsibilities of the ministry, the pastoral problems, the decisions that have to be made, are just more enormous than one man is capable of handling physically, mentally, and emotionally. The strongest of leaders, left on his own, will quickly burn out.

Recall the godly advice that Moses received from his father-in-law, Jethro, in Exodus 18. After viewing Moses exercising his single office of leadership over the people of God for just one day, Jethro came to the clear conclusion (verses 17 & 18): *"What you are doing is not good. [18] You and the people with you will certainly wear yourselves out, for the thing is too heavy for you. You are not able to do it alone.*" And with Jethro's suggestion, the first recorded practice of delegating authority to others in the church came into being, on the basic problem area of potential burnout. Not only is it Biblical to govern the church with a plurality of officers; it is also very wise and prudent and results in a much better level of leadership being exercised for the people.

But on the other extreme, it is possible to delegate and, ultimately, to dissipate the responsibility of leadership too much. Such is the case in a pure democracy, or in a church that is governed almost totally by congregational rule. In this style of church government, a congregation will decide almost every single issue that comes up. Not only how much to pay the pastor, but what color to paint the junior high Sunday school class – by a majority vote of the entire congregation assembled for a "business meeting." In this process, each person has an equal vote and thus shares in the rule of the church. Actually, this form of government results in a number of serious problems, even looked at purely from a sociological perspective.

To begin with, while it may appear on the surface to be some sort of idealistic democracy in which the will of God and the leading of the Spirit ultimately bring about the proper decision every time, as a matter of practice the nature of original sin (sin that remains even in the lives of church members) has a way of developing rivalries, factions, and splits in groups of people. The natural human tendency is to group – to find people who feel pretty much the way you do about certain issues, and to even seek to exercise influence within that group. In this sort of rule, it frequently becomes the case that one particular group – one faction – gains control, exercising the real power in the church; and others feel left out, discouraged, and in many cases decide to leave the church because no one respects their ideas or advice. In other words, their group is not in power.

Another problem with this form of congregational rule is that frequently, even when there is a group actually in power, many decisions do not get made, or get postponed, or some poor decisions are reached. In a large-group process, some people are very reluctant to speak their mind openly and freely. At meetings such as this, people with very good ideas – ideas that, if shared with the congregation, might provide godly, Biblical solutions to issues before the group – decide not to speak for a variety of reasons. They are bashful. They are afraid of rejection. They are lacking confidence in their judgment or knowledge or abilities. Whatever. In my experience working with churches that function with a congregational form of government, there have always been deep levels of frustration in the church of things that need to be done but just not getting accomplished.

Not that the rule by a group of Elders automatically solves every problem. But it has the potential for being the most effective. And it certainly has been shown in this book to be the one most in line with the teaching of the Scriptures. Just on the surface, the benefits of rule by a plurality of Elders are clear. Instead of giving just one strong leader – one individual – all the power, the authority is vested in a number of leaders. This provides for a greater safeguard against abuses of authority. This provides for a distribution of the burden of the ministry. This provides for the strength of one person to fill in where another person has a weakness. This provides for mutually sharing gifts so that all the needed areas of leadership are covered.

At this point let me make several specific remarks about how this plurality works out with Teaching Elders and Ruling Elders. Recall we have demonstrated that these men are in the same office. The difference is only in some specialized functions of laboring in the Word and doctrine, particularly preaching and the administration of the sacraments on the part of the Teaching Elder.

In the plurality of Elders in the local church, how do Teaching Elders and Ruling Elders work together? Our basic principle is that each of them has equal authority. Each one has an equal vote in matters that are to be decided. The opinions, the ideas of each one, should be treated as equally valid. This means that the Teaching Elder should not assume that he knows more Bible or more doctrine or more church polity than do the Ruling Elders. And by the same token, the Ruling Elders should not think that just because they are in the "business world" they have a better handle on making "business decisions" in the church. There should be a clear understanding developed among the men, Teaching and Ruling Elders alike, that they do indeed have what has come to be known as parity in the office of Elder.

In most Presbyterian denominations, including the PCA, the pastor – the senior Minister of the Word; the Teaching Elder with the overall responsibility for preaching in the church – is required to take on the role of moderating the meetings of Elders in the local church. There are several good reasons for this tradition, even though we must remember it is merely that

– a tradition. In almost every case, the Teaching Elder is out-numbered by Ruling Elders, and so in moderating the meeting he in a sense protects the balance – the parity – in the two functional parts of the office. Also, in most cases it is the Minister of the Word who is involved in the day-to-day, nuts-and-bolts operations of the church and is therefore in the best position to draw up the agenda, to field the incoming questions and correspondence, and to do much of the legwork required for such a meeting.

Hopefully it will also be the Teaching Elder who is most recently and thoroughly trained in the polity of the church. At least this should be the case, although it is my increasing observation that young men coming out of seminaries today are less and less knowledgeable about church government and will, in the long run, end up with problems in their ministries because they have failed to obtain or understand the needed training in this area.

Let's shift gears now in our discussion of power and authority and talk about how this plurality of Elders relates to others in the church – in particular, how the Elders are to relate to the congregation as a whole, how they relate to the Deacons, and how they relate to other organized groups in the church.

First, how do the Elders relate to the congregation? First and foremost is the principle that it is the congregation who selects the officers in the first place. We see this in Acts, Chapter 6, when the first Deacons were elected in the church in Jerusalem. We see it also in Acts, Chapter 1, where the early church is faced with the responsibility of electing a replacement for Judas among the twelve apostles. We also see the appointment or choosing of Elders in several of the New Testament churches. In Acts 14, Paul and Barnabas are involved in this process in Lystra, Iconium, and Antioch. In the Pastoral Epistles we see Timothy involved in Ephesus and Titus in Crete.

It is important to note that the New Testament evidence does not give us a clear command to hold "elections" as we know them today. In fact, in Acts 1 and Acts 6, the choice seems to be made by lot, with the assumption that the Holy Spirit was involved in that choice. There are some who would advocate the casting of lots in the church even today – that the total number of qualified men for any given office be placed on some sort of slate or list and that a system of casting lots be developed to choose from among them. I am not one who advocates this form, but at the same time we must be careful not to allow the process of elections to become some sort of popularity contest either.

Also, in setting up Elders in the churches of the New Testament, we sometimes see them being appointed. Particularly do we see this in Acts 14 and in Titus 1. These are probably best understood as "church planting" situations, where there is not a group of Elders already in the area to carry on this process, and so one or two men are given the authority to do this. This happens even today in some church planting situations, especially on the mission field.

But the principle underlying this discussion is that no matter how it works out, it is the congregation who chooses, who elects, who selects their officers. It is not up to the officers to decide who the continuing officers are to be to join them in the ministry.

Now then, if the congregation elects the Elders, does it also follow that they then are representatives of the congregation, and are to vote in ways that suit those people who have elected them? After all, this is the way we do it in our democratic republic that we call America. However, in the church of Jesus the Elders are not chosen as representatives of the people. The church is a monarchy and the Elders are the representatives of King Jesus. Over and over again the Bible teaches us that the church belongs to God. It is Jesus who is the head of the church. And the Elders are not to be viewed as representatives of the people. They are in fact representatives of Jesus. They are under-shepherds to the Great Shepherd. They are magistrates of the King. And the decisions they render must come from the process of deciding what it is that Jesus would have in his church, rather than what the people want in the church.

Hopefully these two things will be the same. For if the people are in fact loyal to their Lord and Savior, they will also want what Jesus wants for the church. But if a conflict were ever to arise, it is important that the Elders recognize that their role, their function, their task is to represent Jesus and to discern and to carry out his will for the church.

I also hope it goes without saying that the Elders will take the needs of the people into consideration in all of their decisions. They cannot exercise authority in some sort of vacuum, ignorant of or immune to the feelings and desires and needs of the people in the church. And so to do this, the Elders must know the people. They must be with their people, just as a shepherd is with his sheep. They must be concerned about the well-being of their people, just as a father is concerned about his family. I am convinced that if Elders are chosen from men who meet the spiritual qualifications we will be discussing in a later chapter and that, if they approach their ministry in the ways we have been discussing, they will be successful in meeting the desires of both Jesus for his church and the people in the church.

As to the relationship of the Elders to the Deacons, we will be covering that in more detail in the chapter on Deacons because it is important to understand the differences between Elders and Deacons before we can understand how these offices relate to each other.

As far as other groups and committees are concerned, I believe we can set forth at least some basic principles at this point. Let's use for illustration purposes the budget committee of the church. We could use the music committee or the Christian Education committee – or any other committee, for that matter – but don't you agree that it is in matters of finances that many interpersonal and inter-group problems often arise in the church? So let's use the budget committee as our example.

Using the Presbyterian Church in America as our model, according to the PCA Book of Church Order it is the duty and responsibility of the Elders to approve and adopt the budget of the church. This is not something given to the congregation on which to vote. It is the Elders' responsibility. In an attempt to maintain good communications with the congregation, the Elders may wisely set up a budget committee, made up of several Deacons who get involved in financial management in the church, and even representatives from other important groups such as Christian Education, worship, youth work, etc. And this committee would be assigned the task of bringing in recommendations to the Elders as to what the next year's budget might be.

I suppose one possible way for the Elders to relate to this committee is to establish it, let it do its work, let it report its recommendations, and then just totally ignore it and come to their own conclusions. I think everyone would agree that this would be very foolish. Why even bother to appoint a committee to seek advice if this were to be the approach? And so that must be our first rule. Elders should never seek recommendations and advice from the congregation if it is not their intention to take that advice into consideration. There must be a valid reason that they want and need that advice. It may be an area that affects so many people in the church that they need a broad-based input (such as is the case with the annual budget). Or it may be an area in which the Elders are uncertain as to how to proceed. It might be an area in which the Scriptures are silent, and they want to reach a consensus that is agreeable to the entire church. Whatever the reason, the Elders should appoint a committee only when they intend to listen to the recommendations and take their advice under real consideration.

Another important point to consider is that Elders should never appoint a committee and not give them guidelines to follow. For instance, perhaps the Elders know that the pastor has a definite need in his family that will require at least a $3,000 raise in the next year or he would be unable to continue as pastor. It would be utter foolishness not to pass that information on to the committee, for if they brought in a recommendation much too low, the Elders would then be faced with the problem of either overruling the committee (and therefore seeming to be very arbitrary) or losing their pastor. Any committee is only as good as the guidelines and information and ground rules they have to work with. It is important for the Elders to give the committees as much information and to maintain communication to the very best possible degree.

Also, if the Elders do find a need to change anything in the recommendation before approving and adopting the budget – perhaps some new information or new opportunity comes up after the committee reports back – there must be a clear communication of the reasons for this change to the committee, and this communication should come prior to the decisions being announced to the rest of the congregation. How would you like to be a member of the budget committee and walk into church one Sunday to find the approved budget for next year on the table ready to be picked up by the entire congregation and there were major changes about which you knew nothing? I think you will agree this is not the way the Elders should work with committees.

We could go on and on with illustrations such as this, but I believe it is clear by now that the exercise of power and authority in the church on the part of the leaders – the Elders – is a very important and, indeed, a very complex issue. It is important to understand not only who exercises leadership in the church, but also how they are to exercise that leadership.

When we get to the chapter on qualifications for office, I believe you will see then why it is so important that Elders have some very special character traits and attributes that will permit them to function in this very special office of leadership in the church.

CHAPTER 8

Church Discipline

In our last few chapters we have been discussing the various functions and tasks of Elders in the church, and we gave some warnings about how those functions and tasks should (and shouldn't) be carried out in the exercise of authority. In this chapter we come to what in the minds of many is the most crucial task and, at the same time, the most neglected task of Elders in the church today: church discipline.

While all the initial Protestant reformers agreed that the preaching of the Word of God and the faithful administration of the Sacraments of the church were marks that identified a true church, it was John Knox, founder of Presbyterianism who first insisted that Church Discipline was a third, necessary mark – without which no church could be considered a true one.

In thinking back to our basic function illustrations of a father, a shepherd, and a ruler, it should logically follow that one of the important tasks of the Elder is guarding and promoting both the purity and the peace of the church. Recall Paul's exhortations to Timothy and Titus, as well as to the Ephesian Elders to keep out heresy, to admonish, to shepherd. Certainly all of this involves the exercise of some sort of control, some kind of discipline. The twin goals should always be the same: the purity of the church and peace in the church. But the Elder is always tasked with sorting out exactly how this happens and which takes priority. In every decision, in every vote taken on the Session, there is an element of church discipline involved, and so it is crucial that this be clearly understood by all.

There is a basic truth in the Bible that when the issues of purity and peace come into tension (in other words, one decision could provide more peace and another decision could provide more purity), the Bible tells us clearly which one is to prevail. Let's look first at the prophet Jeremiah, Chapter 6, verses 13 and 14: *"For from the least to the greatest of them, everyone is greedy for unjust gain; and from prophet to priest, everyone deals falsely. [14] They have healed the wound of my people lightly, saying, 'Peace, peace,' when there is no peace."*

Jeremiah's lament in this passage is that the leaders of the people of God simply give lip service to the subject of peace. Although they keep saying that everything in God's kingdom is peaceful, the truth is there is no peace at all. And what is the cause of the lack of peace? You have to look back to verses 30-31 of Chapter 5: *"An appalling and horrible thing has happened in the land: the prophets prophesy falsely, and the priests rule at their direction; my people love to have it so, but what will you do when the end comes?"*

The problem in Jerusalem was that there was no purity. None of the leaders of God's people followed the teachings of scripture in conducting their office. None of the people of God demanded leaders who would follow the Lord. And without this sort of Biblical purity, the result was a lack of peace.

Paul sees the same thing in the New Testament. In Romans, Chapter 2, verses 5 through 11, we have a long passage but one well worth examining. *"But because of your hard and impenitent heart you are storing up wrath for yourself on the day of wrath when God's righteous judgment will be revealed. [6] he will render to each one according to his works: [7] to those who by patience in well-doing seek for glory and honor and immortality, he will give eternal life; [8] but for those who are self-seeking and do not obey the truth, but obey unrighteousness, there will be wrath and fury. [9] There will be tribulation and distress for every human being who does evil, the Jew first and also the Greek, [10] but glory and honor and peace for everyone who does good, the Jew first and also the Greek. [11] For God shows no partiality."*

Paul, as usual, has a very logical train of thought in this passage. And that train of thought goes like this: If someone practices truth and follows good, then the result will be peace – peace now and the peace of eternal life. But if someone does not practice truth and follow good, then the result will be just the opposite of peace, it will be wrath. Paul sees this basic priority in the eyes of God, as taught by the Scriptures. Purity must always take priority over peace, because peace results from purity.

Hopefully there will be very few decisions in the church in which Elders will have to choose between purity and peace. Most of the time, by choosing the Biblical way – by following good and truth – the Elders will be effective in bringing about peace. One clear way in which this works is in controlling membership into the visible church. It is the responsibility of the Elders to examine people who seek to become members. And they should examine them to be sure that they make a credible profession of faith in Jesus, that they understand the basic issues of Christianity, and that they themselves are partakers of that "so great salvation" which Jesus came to purchase.

As well as making a credible profession of faith, there must be in the lives of people applying for membership no flagrant sin that contradicts their confession. For example, if someone were to come to the Elders to seek membership and gave a profession of faith, and at the same time admitted to being a practicing homosexual, they would have to be denied membership. The continuing practice of this clear Biblical sin denies the profession of faith. In a case such as this the Elders would have to choose purity, calling homosexuality a sin, as the Bible does, over "peace" (the peace that would result from overlooking Biblical truth in order to satisfy the desires of some people).

I believe, however, that you can see from this example that this would not be true peace at all. It would fit the cry of Jeremiah that the priests were saying: *"Peace, peace. when there was no peace."* Just trying to keep people satisfied and happy while ignoring the clear teachings of the Bible will never result in peace in the church of Jesus.

And so in the task of exercising discipline over membership in the church, Elders are performing what to my way of thinking may be the most crucial task they have. Before we go much further, let me say very clearly that discipline is not just a negative term. Many people think of it that way. When they think of discipline, they think of punishment. But such is not necessarily the case. There are some very positive aspects of discipline, including instruction, education, admonition, and counseling.

In Hebrews 10:24-25, the author gives us a taste of this: *"And let us consider how to stir up one another to love and good works, [25] not neglecting to meet together, as is the habit of some, but encouraging one another, and all the more as you see the Day drawing near."* The author sees the clear need for this positive sort of discipline – for spurring one another on, for encouraging one another – as a vital work of the church.

This positive aspect of discipline is not the exclusive work of the Elders, but rather is the work of the whole church. The passage in Hebrews is addressed to all who assemble together. Paul, in Romans 15:14, says essentially the same thing when he writes: *"I myself am satisfied about you, my brothers, that you yourselves are full of goodness, filled with all knowledge and able to instruct one another."*

But there are times when it becomes necessary to exercise what we would call the negative aspect of discipline. And when that is necessary, then the Elders normally get involved to fulfill this task. And when is formal church discipline necessary? Well, the necessity of church discipline is so closely related to the purpose of church discipline that we must look at these two topics together. The Bible gives us at least four major reasons for the necessity and purpose of church discipline.

The first – and in fact the most important one – is to bring glory to God through obedience to his word. That is clearly what God wants, and that is what we must do in the church. Matthew 18:15-19 is generally regarded as the classic text on this subject. In these verses, Jesus is speaking: *"If your brother sins against you, go and tell him his fault, between you and him alone. If he listens to you, you have gained your brother. [16] But if he does not listen, take one or two others along with you, that every charge may be established by the evidence of two or three witnesses. [17] If he refuses to listen to them, tell it to the church. And if he refuses to listen even to the church, let him be to you as a Gentile and a tax collector. [18] Truly, I say to you, whatever you bind on earth shall be bound in heaven, and whatever you loose on earth shall be loosed in heaven. [19] Again I say to you, if two of you agree on earth about anything they ask, it will be done for them by my Father in heaven."*

Jesus is teaching that the exercise of church discipline (first in a positive way by individual members, but ultimately by the church, formally acting through its officers) is so much the will of God that doing it on earth is exactly the same thing as doing it in heaven. In other words, the exercise of discipline by Elders, following Biblical principles, is in fact the exercise of discipline by God himself.

Several other things happen when we are obedient to God in this matter, which themselves become part of the necessity and purpose of church discipline. The first of these is that discipline will reclaim offenders. Jesus begins his own teaching by saying that if you work the process and the sinning brother listens, *"you have gained your brother."* In other words, you have reclaimed him for the church. In the most serious case of 1 Corinthians 5, where a man had to be excommunicated from the church, Paul says in verse 5: *"You are to deliver this man to Satan for the destruction of the flesh, so that his spirit may be saved in the day of the Lord."* You see, even in the most extreme cases of discipline the purpose is still to reclaim the offender.

90

Of course, the exercise of church discipline results in maintaining purity in the church. We have looked at that extensively already. But another effect is to deter others from sin. First Timothy 5:20 seems very clear on this point: *"As for those who persist in sin, rebuke them in the presence of all, so that the rest may stand in fear."* Exercising discipline must never be hidden from the rest of the congregation. There is a proper way to deal with it publicly spelled out in the various Books of Church Order.

The next categories to examine are the forms or various modes or types of church discipline. The most basic one we have looked at a number of times. It is simply admonishing a brother, telling him that something is in fact a sin. That, of course, is where Jesus tells us in Matthew 18 to begin.

The next step up would be to reprove, to rebuke, to convince, or to convict – all of which are appropriate English translations of the same Greek word. This word is found in a number of passages in the New Testament. Frequently this will take on the form of something specific along with a verbal admonishment. Perhaps a member may be denied membership privileges for a time, being suspended from the sacraments of the church, until there is repentance from a certain sin. Sometimes it means that an officer may be deposed or suspended from exercising an office in the church because of sin. There are a variety of ways in which concrete, visible action can be taken to demonstrate the seriousness of discipline in the church.

Of course the final step is that which we call excommunication. That is the end result in Jesus' own teaching in Matthew 18. That is also what happened to the man discussed in 1

Corinthians 5. Ultimately, if there is no repentance, the individual must be removed from membership totally – excommunicated from the congregation.

This does not mean that once someone is excommunicated he cannot again be restored to the church in the future. Recall, restoration is one of the purposes of discipline. That can even happen with excommunication. In 2 Corinthians 2:6-8, Paul touches on this when he writes concerning the same man excommunicated in 1 Corinthians 5: *"For such a one, this punishment by the majority is enough, [7] so you should rather turn to forgive and comfort him, or he may be overwhelmed by excessive sorrow. [8] So I beg you to reaffirm your love for him."*

You see, once there is repentance, there must be this reaffirmation of love and restoration to fellowship in the church. Having personally gone through this process with people a number of times in the past, I can attest to the joy that comes from this end result.

The next question frequently asked is: "When do you exercise discipline? Everyone sins, so how do we decide whom to discipline and whom to let off?" Actually, putting the question in this way sets up a false dichotomy. No one should be let off. Every sin should at least be admonished. But there are times when you must proceed beyond informal admonishment and take more formal action. In the illustrations we have already looked at in the Bible and in several other passages, it appears that there are several basic issues that must always be dealt with to the fullest.

First, whenever Christian love is violated, there must be discipline. Love of God, love of one another, is so much a part of the Christian life that it cannot be overlooked when it is violated. To such an extent is this true that in marriage, adultery (the violation of love) is the only grounds for divorce recognized in the Bible.

Also, whenever Christian unity is broken, action must be taken. The church is one body. All members are important and needed. Anyone who breaks that unity, who causes division, must be dealt with.

Of course if Christian law or Biblical truth is violated, there must be discipline as well. Any gross sin or heresy cannot be ignored. This is particularly true if the sin becomes publicly known. It is one thing for a person to believe to himself that a certain doctrine or Biblical truth is right or wrong. But to practice or teach this publicly in the church, contrary to the love and unity expressed in the body of Christ, would indeed call for discipline.

There are many objections that have been raised over the years against the practice of church discipline. Normally these objections are vocalized as the result of not really understanding the nature and purpose of discipline. For instance, some would say that the practice of discipline could cause division in the church. Well, yes it could. So could preaching the Bible consistently. So could requiring Sunday school teachers to believe and teach the standards of the church. But remember, obedience must take priority over peace if the two cannot possibly be reconciled. And ultimately the only true peace and true unity you can have comes as the result of demanding purity.

Another objection goes like this: "To discipline someone would be judging them. After all, doesn't the Bible say *"Judge not, that you be not judged"* (Matt 7:1). I recall a case in a former pastorate when the Session was meeting to act in discipline in a particular case. One Elder who just did not comprehend the Biblical necessity of taking action came into the meeting. The men were all sitting around a beautiful oak table in the church's conference room, and this Elder walked up to the table, took out a handful of stones from his suit pocket, threw them in the middle of the table, and said, "Let he who is without sin cast the first stone." And then he walked out of the room.

Certainly none of those Elders sitting at the table were perfect, were without any sin themselves. But the Bible calls upon leaders in the church to make judgments, to make decisions. And so the real warning is that the judgments should not be hypocritical. Don't demand something of a member that is not also demanded, even more intensely, of all the Elders. But nowhere does the Bible say that no judgments are to be made at all.

One very important objection that must be answered is this: "If the Pastor and the Elders intend to practice discipline, how can we trust them to discuss our problems?" This is indeed a serious concern. And so it is very important that Elders keep strict confidentiality in every case of discipline or counseling in the church (including not telling their wives!).

And if a Minister of the Word (or any other Elder) is counseling and can in a one-on-one relationship follow the injunctions of Matthew 18 and reclaim the sinner in this way, then there need be no further mention of the case. But any blatant failure to repent of sin when it is pointed out must be dealt with for-mally. Actually, by this time it almost always becomes public knowledge anyway, so the issue of confidentiality becomes a moot point.

I suspect that people will always have some objections to dis-cipline. I know when I was a child growing up I didn't appreci-ate it at all. But now as an adult, as a father, as an Elder, I under-stand and appreciate it. I can't say I like it any better, but I see its necessity, its purpose, its value. And most importantly I see its Biblical demands, and those demands I must follow. I would exhort every other Elder to follow them as well

CHAPTER 9

The Function and Tasks of Deacons

For the past several chapters we have been concentrating on the Biblical office of Elder. We have looked at the Elders' function, the Elders' tasks, the relationship of power and authority as exercised by Elders in the church; and then in the last chapter we really zeroed in on a very important task of Elders – that of church discipline.

In this chapter we want to turn our attention to the other continuing office in the church today, the office of Deacon. Recall that classic text we discovered in Paul's letter to the church at Philippi, Philippians 1:1. In giving his greetings to the church, as was the custom in writing letters in those days, Paul specified that two groups of leaders in the church receive his special greetings: the Bishops and the Deacons.

So far we have been able to see who the Bishops were; they are what we today call Elders. But who are the Deacons? Surely they were a separate class of officer, but apparently not every church had them. Several churches we see much of in the New Testament, such as Ephesus, have no mention of this special office. But this church in Philippi had Deacons. Were there any other churches we can determine that had these officers?

Although the actual word, the title of the office, is not used, I believe we can see that the church in Jerusalem had Deacons as well. In fact, it is the strong probability that it was in Jerusalem that this very office originated, which would account for the reason that the title was not used, since the office was just coming into being. The name, the title for the office, may not have been determined or put into general use at the time.

In Acts 6:1-7 we can see what was going on in the church in Jerusalem that required this special function of Deacon: *"Now in these days when the disciples were increasing in number, a complaint by the Hellenists arose against the Hebrews because their widows were being neglected in the daily distribution. [2] And the twelve summoned the full number of the disciples and said, "It is not right that we should give up preaching the word of God to serve tables. [3] Therefore, brothers, pick out from among you seven men of good repute, full of the Spirit and of wisdom, whom we will appoint to this duty. [4] But we will devote ourselves to prayer and to the ministry of the word." [5] And what they said pleased the whole gathering, and they chose Stephen, a man full of faith and of the Holy Spirit, and Philip, and Prochorus, and Nicanor, and Timon, and Parmenas, and Nicolaus, a proselyte of Antioch. [6] These they set before the apostles, and they prayed and laid their hands on them. [7] And the word of God continued to increase, and the number of the disciples multiplied greatly in Jerusalem, and a great many of the priests became obedient to the faith."*

The scene in this chapter is very early in the life of the church, not long after Jesus' ascension and not long after the church began to grow quickly. In fact, there were a number of people in Jerusalem who had remained there after the feast of Passover (during which the crucifixion took place). These people were involved in all the exciting events following Jesus' death and resurrection. Many of these people were not only from out of town, but they were from a different culture. They were Hellenists, or Greek-speaking Jews, as opposed to being Hebraic Jews, those who spoke Hebrew and Aramaic, as had Jesus.

In Acts 6:1 we see that these Greek-speaking Jews were complaining about a problem. The problem was that the Greek-speaking widows were not being cared for in the same way; as the Aramaic-speaking widows. Notice right away that it was assumed by the early church that people in need were to be cared for. This was not something new, something that was uniquely Christian. Ministry of mercy has a long tradition, going back to the Garden of Eden and being fulfilled throughout Israel in the Old Testament – at least as long as Israel was following her God.

And so it was assumed by these Hellenistic Jews that the widows were to be cared for by the community of believers. Apparently something had gone wrong. They were not getting their fair share. Verse 2 speaks of a group of men known as *"the Twelve."* This refers, of course, to the Apostles, but in this case the word Apostle is not used. Very possibly this implies that they were not functioning at this point as Apostles, but rather as Elders exercising oversight in the church. In any case, the Twelve did not need to decide whether or not the church ought to care for those in need; that was never the issue. Rather, the only decision to be made was how to go about it.

We must not overlook this fact too quickly. The care for the needy is an important ministry in the church of Jesus. And in our day and age it is something that far too many churches have in fact overlooked. We should not worry about deciding whether or not to be involved in mercy ministries. We must simply decide the best way to go about the work, which is what the Jerusalem church is doing in Acts 6.

If in fact the Twelve were functioning as Elders at this point, notice the assumption is that it was their responsibility. They felt the pressure on them to solve the problem. They didn't point fingers at anyone else for not doing what they were supposed to do. It was clearly their responsibility. And they recognized that there was a very good reason why it was not being cared for sufficiently and consistently – because there was so much to be done by the Elders (by the Twelve) in terms of the ministry of the Word of God, in ruling and in teaching.

So the Twelve came up with a solution that resulted in their delegating what was initially and basically their own responsibility. They delegated it to another group of people. Seven men who were spiritually qualified were found to take care of this mercy ministry, and they were set apart for special service in the church.

There are several interesting points to take notice of in this incident. First, all seven of these men had Greek names. They were most likely chosen from among the Greek-speaking Jews, who would best know the specific needs of the widows from their own community, their own culture. It is a very practical decision, and one that we can learn from yet today. It is more natural for people to be involved in ministries with those of their own culture, their own background. For instance, it is very difficult for whites to be involved in mercy ministry in black communities, even when their intentions are as pure as possible. That is why cross-cultural missions are so very difficult. That is why there is such a strong impetus to build up indigenous churches as soon as possible to carry out ministry within their own cultures.

Another point to be seen here is that it was not just the Twelve (the Elders) who made the decision as to who would fulfill this special office. The decision was left to the choice of the entire congregation. This is another important lesson for church government. Election of officers is up to the people, not just those in leadership deciding who will join them in some sort of special club.

There is one more important application to make from this passage. It involves the result of having Deacons function in the church. Verse 7: *"And the word of God continued to increase, and the number of the disciples multiplied greatly in Jerusalem, and a great many of the priests became obedient to the faith."*

It is not only evangelism that brings about church growth. From this illustration we see that it is also mercy ministries, caring for people in need. My bet is that those Jewish priests who became believers did so when they came under the influence of godly Christians demonstrating their love for other people. It was through seeing this demonstration of love that they were able to come to the conclusion that there was truth to this new religion that Christianity was in fact from God.

Another major point to learn from this passage is to see the clear difference between the function of Elders (as demonstrated by the Twelve) and the function of Deacons (as demonstrated by the Seven). We decided earlier that if there is one term that describes for us what Elders do, it was oversight. And surely that is what the Twelve wanted to continue to do: to minister the Word, to exercise spiritual oversight over the entire congregation.

But what was it that the Seven were doing? What one word can we use to describe their function? Verse 2 contains the answer, in the term translated *"to serve tables."* The root of this word is the same that we find in the word for the office of Deacon. The verb form is "diakonos," which means "service." (In fact, this is the same word that is used in the Gospels when describing Jesus as the model of being a 'servant.')

And so it is very easy to see how these seven have come to be understood as the first Deacons in the church – because their main function was that of service. Remember that distinction; it is very important. Elders are involved in oversight. Deacons are involved in service.

Given that basic Biblical picture of the essential function of a Deacon, what can we say about the various tasks that will flesh out the function of service? I believe we can find in the Bible at least four separate, distinguishable tasks that are important for Deacons everywhere. The first of these is the one we have already been looking at in the context of the development of the office itself: mercy ministries. This should be the primary task of every Deacon, and certainly of every Board of Deacons in every Biblical church – to provide mercy to those in need, particularly those with physical and economic needs. This includes not only those within the congregation; it should extend into the broader community outside the church as well.

The task of mercy ministry can take on a number of different forms. A Deacon can be involved in visiting the sick along with the Elders of the church. They can visit the poor, the elderly, the shut-in. In some communities there are people with very special needs. In one church in which I served, we had a number of women whose husbands were on active duty in the military and who were away from home for long periods on military assignments. There the Deacons had an excellent ministry in taking care of special needs for these families. These ladies were not poor, were not what we would normally think of as "needy." But with the husband and father gone for long periods of time, there was much the Deacons could do to help out in the absence of the "man of the house."

The second main task for Deacons involves the giving of the church. This task we usually refer to as stewardship. It is an important task, but must be seen as a secondary task to that of mercy ministries. Deacons can and should be involved in encouraging the people of the God to give and to aid them in this process by helping them collect and distribute those gifts. Most often in Presbyterian circles, you will find a Deacon serving as a treasurer for a church – certainly an appropriate task.

Another task that falls to the responsibility of Deacons is the care for real property that the church may own or lease. This involves repair and maintenance of buildings, plumbing, heating, air-conditioning, what have you. It also deals with the maintenance of grounds, landscaping, cutting the grass, etc. Now, the Deacons don't have to do all of these various tasks, but certainly they are delegated the responsibility to see that they are accomplished.

One additional task that falls to Deacons is the idea of "helps." This is one of the gifts listed in Romans 12, and it seems to fall best in the category of tasks for Deacons. There are many very practical things that are required to be accomplished in a church in the 21st century, and the church must place responsibility for them somewhere. Many of these "helps" can properly be viewed as the work of the Deacons. For instance, ushering, setting up chairs and tables for a church supper, obtaining equipment for use in work projects – many such errands and tasks can properly be under the watchful eyes of the Board of Deacons.

In an earlier chapter, we discussed the use of power and authority on the part of Elders, and we mentioned briefly that in their relationship with Deacons there is frequently a chance for problems to spring up. We want to zero in on that issue more deeply now in this chapter.

As we have seen, the very office of Deacon was a delegated office from the Elders. So it logically follows that Deacons fall under the oversight, control, and review of the Elders of the church. We must not picture Presbyterian church government as having two legislative bodies, such as we have in the United States. It is not analogous to the Senate and the House of Representatives, each making decisions that affect the governing of our nation. Not at all. Deacons do not make decisions that exercise oversight in the church. They merely carry out the various tasks of service delegated to them in the church.

As an example, let look at the issue of finances. This is one area in which some churches have problems today. In these congregations, there is a sort of third office developed that is given some of the responsibility that properly belongs to Deacons (or even to Elders). It is usually called the office of "Trustee." Nowhere does the Bible ever refer to a Trustee. In fact, this very term comes from the English system of law that places the responsibility for care of funds and of property in the hands of "trustees." This is one of the clearest examples you can find of the secular, civil form of governing people becoming a model for the church.

But in other cases, just the opposite is true. So much are the Deacons given responsibility for finances that it is almost as if they have total control over anything having to do with money. In such cases, the Elders just make "spiritual" decisions. But do you see the fallacy of such a position? He who controls the purse strings in the church in fact exercises oversight and rules the church. And to abdicate that entire role to the Deacons puts them in the business of exercising oversight, of ruling, rather than remaining in the Biblical model of performing service.

Although most of the functional tasks of handling finances and budgets can be delegated, ultimately the Elders must have control of the budget. In fact, in the PCA it is spelled out that only the Elders can approve and adopt the budget. The Deacons may make recommendations, and it certainly would be wise and prudent for the Elders to listen to this advice. But in the long run, the decision-making process must remain with the Elders.

I personally believe that the best way for all this to be accomplished – and for the Deacons not to feel that they are being left out of the process – is for the very best possible communication link to be set up between the two boards. Certainly at least one Elder (and my own personal suggestion is that at least one Teaching Elder, preferably the pastor or an associate pastor with special responsibilities, plus one Ruling Elder) ought to meet with the Deacons every time they conduct their business. This provides for two-way communications. The Elders can communicate the decisions or desires of the Elders, and the Deacons can then in a very personal, one-on-one way communicate their advice and recommendation. Much care needs to be taken in the church that this communication – this relationship – remains viable at all times.

There is one final task that I would like to discuss in this unit concerning deacons. And it is the subject of church-based counseling. It is becoming more and more popular in Presbyterian circles today to view the role of counselors as a "Diaconal" function – to see it as a work of mercy or service. But I must confess that I have a real problem with this concept. As one who was involved in counseling on a professional level for over two decades, licensed and a member of a clinical society for family counselors, I know what counseling entails. And certainly in the context of the church it is far more than a Diaconal function.

A Christian counselor in a very real sense must be gifted to teach the Scriptures to a counselee. And in many, many cases, particularly with pastoral counseling in the organized church, there is a need to exercise authority and rule over the person receiving the counseling. I am convinced that the task of counseling is a proper task for a Pastor-Teacher – for an Elder – and not something that should be subsumed under the role of Deacons in the church.

There certainly are many sorts of counseling issues that are really just "helps," as we have already discussed them. And so the Deacons are not totally separated from this area. In fact, every Christian has responsibility to conduct what Dr. Larry Crabbe calls "Counseling by Encouragement." This certainly is something that Deacons could and should be involved in – but not the formal counseling that has become so popular in our country. Anyone wanting to carry on this kind of counseling inside the church should be gifted, called, and ordained as an Elder, or at the very least employed in a counseling center under the authority of the Session.

Let me say once again in closing that even though we have spent only one chapter on the office of Deacon, this is not to be taken as a way of subtly saying this is not an important office. It is very important. However, in deciding how to divide the time up in covering the very many items that needed to be included in this book, it was my best judgment to spend considerably more time on the office of Elder, because it is here that the ultimate future of every Presbyterian church stands or falls. A godly, qualified, functioning Board of Deacons can do much to maintain the health of and support the growth of any church, and my prayer is that your church has just such a board of Deacons. But ultimately a church can exist without this office, at which time all of these functions and tasks then become the responsibility of the Elders to carry out. It should be quite obvious that anyone who is an Elder certainly will want to have a group of fine, godly Deacons in his church.

CHAPTER 10

The Role Of Women In The Church

This chapter is one that, if I thought I could get away with it, I wouldn't even include in the book. If there were other issues that have come up previously in the book with which the reader had differences of opinion, you probably would just pass it off as that – a difference of opinion. But here, at the beginning of the 21st century, there is probably no single issue that can raise as much discussion – and in some quarters as much dissension – as the issue of the role of women in the church. Families have been split, local congregations torn asunder, and denominations broken into pieces on this particular issue.

But we cannot avoid it. Surely if our entire goal in this series has been to seek to understand what the Bible itself has to teach about church government – about how and why and who exercises leadership in the church – then we must come to the discussion, sooner or later, of the role of women.

We have wanted all along not to make our judgments based on what is current practice or what is practical or what is historical. We have wanted to make our judgments on what the Bible teaches, and so we must continue along those same lines as we look at this issue.

I want to divide the question into two main parts. First, we will look at the role of women in the teaching/ruling functions of the church. In other words, can a woman function in the office of Elder, as we have described it in this series? Then we will turn our attention to the office of Deacon and ask the same question again: Can a woman serve in the office of Deacon, according to the Scriptures?

First, let's look at the role of women in the teaching and ruling functions of the church. And this in itself is a major question in our generation in many churches. Nearly all so-called "mainline" Protestant denominations in America ordain women to teaching/ruling offices, and even the Roman Catholic Church in the more "desolate" parts of the world are allowing women to serve in this capacity to some degree. Actually the position that women may serve in the teaching/ruling functions in the church is also held by some otherwise evangelical denominations that would even agree with the doctrine of infallibility of the Scriptures.

Whether mainline or evangelical, this position is usually based on the view that the New Testament is simply expressing the culture of its day and it is not normative for us today in the 21st century. This is supposedly similar to the Bible's position on master/slave relationships.

When we turn to the Scriptures, however, we will see that the view held by the Presbyterian Church in America and several other evangelical denominations that oppose the ordination of women to any teaching/ruling function in the church is based on other than cultural principles. Basically speaking, these principles are as follows:

There is "an image equality" between men and women. As we look at the Bible we find that all human beings are created in the image of God. Genesis 1:27 tells us: *"So God created man in his own image, in the image of God he created him; male and female he created them."* This is an important, basic theme. Because in the Fall it is the image of God that is marred, that is damaged. But the New Testament picks up this theme and recognizes that this marred image is what is restored and renewed through the work of Jesus.

This is very clear in Paul's Second Letter to the Corinthians, Chapter 5, where he writes, beginning at verse 17: *"Therefore, if anyone is in Christ,* [in other words, if anyone has had the finished work of Jesus applied to his life], he *is a new creation. The old has passed away; behold, the new has come."* Paul is saying that the old, marred image is gone away. We have a new, reconciled image through Christ. Just two chapters earlier Paul had written: *"And we all, with unveiled face, beholding the glory of the Lord, are being transformed into the same image from one degree of glory to another. For this comes from the Lord who is the Spirit."* (2 Cor 3:18)

Clearly this image is restored and renewed through the what Jesus did on the cross. So, seeking to think logically, if both man and woman were created in the image of God, and if the fallen image is restored and renewed through the work of Christ, therefore – in Christ – all are equal in image. And isn't that exactly what Paul writes in Galatians 3:28: *"There is neither Jew nor Greek, there is neither slave nor free, there is neither male nor female, for you are all one in Christ Jesus."* And Peter writes to husbands and tells them that their wives are heirs with them in the future life in Christ. Clearly, therefore, all – men and women – are equal in their renewed and restored image.

But just because we have established the existence of "image equality" it does not necessarily mean that a "role-relationship equality" exists. This is a different issue entirely. Peter even spoke of image equality (in 1 Peter 3:7) in the midst of his teaching on the differences of the role relationships between men and women in marriage. And certainly in this sphere, in the area of marriage, God has established certain specific role relationships.

Now, this role relationship between men and women is not something particularly Christian. It is not even particularly Jewish. It is another creation ordinance, something established by God at creation to provide order for people for all time and in all religions. The passage in Genesis 2:18-25 establishes the first marriage relationship and sets forth the standards, the boundaries. Of course in the New Testament, the Apostle Paul gives us a clearer and more specific set of guidelines in Ephesians 5:22-33. And this role relationship sets forth a position of head-ship for the man over the woman, exercising (in a loving and Biblical way) authority and dominion over the woman in the marriage relationship. Very few individuals reading this book would dispute this clear Biblical truth.

However, the question remains: If there is not a role-relation-ship equality in the sphere of marriage, what about the sphere of the church? Is there a role relationship that applies there as well? In order to answer this question, we must look at one very key passage of Scripture. In virtually every study you will find on the subject of any possible role relationship of men and women in the church, you must deal with this portion of Scripture. And in keeping with this series of studies on church government, we find the passage is in – you guessed it – 1 Timothy. This time it is in Chapter 2, verses 11 through 15.

"Let a woman learn quietly with all submissiveness. [12] I do not permit a woman to teach or to exercise authority over a man; rather, she is to remain quiet. [13] For Adam was formed first, then Eve; [14] and Adam was not deceived, but the woman was deceived and became a transgressor. [15] Yet she will be saved through child-bearing – if they continue in faith and love and holiness, with self-control."

Obviously this passage contains a number of difficult and controversial issues for interpretation. But before we examine the passage itself, let's recall the context. Remember what we said earlier in this book. The purpose of 1 Timothy is to give instructions for life and organization in the visible church. In keeping with this purpose, we must recognize that Paul has written these verses under consideration to teach us something about church organization, so it certainly has a great deal of bearing on the subject matter at hand.

Without going into some of the periphery material in the passage, we can see clearly that Paul prohibits two different things in what he writes. The first is that women may not teach men. Now, we must hasten to add that this prohibition specifically applies to public teaching in the church. We cannot from the context necessarily imply any analogy to other spheres of life. That will have to remain as a discussion for another time. But clearly women are not to teach men in the church.

This is very similar to Paul's instructions given in 1 Corinthians, Chapter 14, verses 33-38. Without reading that entire passage, let us recall that the context involved the practice in the church in Corinth of using a method of question-and-answer model of teaching. Prophets would speak their word of prophecy, and people in the congregation would then ask them questions, and this produced a certain style of teaching in the church. Paul prohibited women from participating in this practice of questioning the prophets. He said (in verse 34): *"the women should keep silent in the churches. For they are not permitted to speak, but should be in submission, as the Law also says."*

This was not a rule that forbade them from participating in worship in other ways. They could clearly pray. They could speak in tongues themselves. It is probable that they even served as prophets. But they could not be involved in the formal teaching process, even to the extent of asking questions, because the questions themselves were designed as teaching elements.

We should also point out that this prohibition in 1 Corinthians and in 1 Timothy does not preclude women from fulfilling the function of teaching other women or children. Titus 2:4 is a helpful reference to support this point. There, Paul encourages older women to *"train the young women to love their husbands and children."* This was, of course, in the context of the formal work of the church.

There is a second prohibition given by Paul in our basic text in 1 Timothy 2. And that is that women may not exercise authority or rule over men. Again, we must remind ourselves that this teaching applies specifically to the public work of the church.

There is not enough evidence in this particular passage to say that women cannot hold civil office or work in supervisory positions over men in the business or education world. But in the church, clearly women may not teach men and may not exercise authority over men.

Now, as we have carefully defined the office of Elder in the church as the office that is responsible for teaching and exercising authority, it becomes very clear that this prohibition means women are not eligible to serve in the office of Elder in the church. They may not be Teaching Elders (Ministers of the Word), and they may not be Ruling Elders, since this is one basic office with a variety of functions. We don't have to worry at this point about the argument in the list of qualifications about whether an Elder being the husband of one wife applies or not; that is not the relevant point. The prohibitions against the specific functions of teaching and exercising oversight, functions that are at the very heart of the office of Elder, make this restriction clear.

Notice that Paul gives several reasons for these prohibitions in the text in 1 Timothy 2. First, Paul sees the order of creation – that Adam was created prior to Eve – as an expression and determination of God's design and order. 1 Corinthians 11, verses 1-16, expands and clarifies this for us.

But notice also that another reason given is that it was the failure of Adam and Eve to follow this creation order that, in effect, brought on the Fall. Eve's giving in to temptation, without being subject to the headship of her husband, and Adam's failure to exercise the protection required of that headship are examples of what happens when the creation order is not followed.

And it is an important point that Paul is making here. He is not giving cultural reasons for these prohibitions. He is not saying that in this society, or in that church, this is the best way to do things. Paul bases his Biblical prohibitions on the order of creation, and they are separate from any cultural issues, either Old Testament or New Testament. So we cannot argue that the role relationship of women in the church is something that applied to churches only in some other generation or period or culture. These prohibitions are set for the entire creation, for all time.

We want now to shift to our second major question. What about the role of women in the church vis-à-vis the office of Deacon? Does the Bible allow for women to function in this office? There is another key passage that we must understand. And again it is in 1 Timothy, this time right in Chapter 3 in the middle of our list of qualifications for officers. Verse 11 reads: *"Their wives* likewise must be dignified, not slanderers, but sober-minded, faithful in all things."* (The ESV footnotes *'Their wives'* with two alternate translations; either just *'Wives'* or just *'Women', which shows the great difficulty in determining what is meant in this verse.)*

The key word in this verse is the one that most translations, such as the King James, NIV, and ESV, translate as "wives." Recall that this verse appears right in the middle of a list of qualifications for Deacons. And these translations show their clear theological conclusion limiting women from the office of Deacon by translating this word as "wives" in this verse. However, in five previous occurrences in the preceding chapter, 1 Timothy 2, this same word is translated "women." Both English words are proper translations of this one Greek word,

116

depending on the context. And to complicate the issue even further, there is no separate word in the Greek to use for 'wives.'

Dr. James Hurley, currently on the faculty of Reformed Theological Seminary in Jackson, Mississippi, wrote a book that I believe is the best modern treatise (sadly now out of print) on the subject of the Bible's view of women, covering far more than our current topic of church government (*Man and Woman In Biblical Perspective*, 1981, Zondervan). In Hurley's treatment of this verse, he gives us several options to choose from that are extremely helpful (as well as providing background for much of the material in this chapter). Hurley points out that all translators have five possible choices concerning the women in view in this verse. They are (1) women in general, (2) wives of Elders and Deacons, (3) wives of Deacons, (4) themselves Deacons, or (5) a group similar to, but distinct from, Deacons (perhaps to be referred to as Deaconesses).

Hurley quickly and properly eliminates the first choice. Paul is talking about church officers, not about people in general. And the location – in the middle of the list for Deacons – makes it very difficult to apply it also to the wives of Elders, so he quickly eliminates the second option. Then he points out this excellent interpretation: "If Paul intended to talk of wives of Deacons, he could easily have made his intention clear by saying 'their wives' or even 'the wives.' Translations wishing to adopt the meaning wives have generally supplied one of the two words. The Biblical text offers no support for this."

Hurley goes on to show that either Options 4 or 5 must be his conclusion (actually, he is closest to Option 4 – that they are in fact Deacons). He points out the clear parallel of the four qualities set forth in verses 8-10 and the four qualities set forth in verse 11, which match up almost perfectly. The men must be worthy of respect; the women also (even the same Greek word is used). The men must not be double-tongued; the women must not be slanderers. The men must not be given to much wine; the women must be sober and temperate. The men must not be pursuing dishonest gain; the women must be trustworthy in all things. Hurley comes to the conclusion that, according to the Bible, women are eligible for the office of Deacon.

With the clearly understood difference between the office of Elder, which is an office of teaching and ruling, and the office of Deacon, which is an office of service, there is nothing in the nature, the function, or the task of being a Deacon that would exclude women as it does with the office of Elder. The Bible teaches in several places that women may carry on special service functions in the church.

In 1 Timothy 5, there is clearly a roll – a board or committee if you will – of widows who have specific service to perform. In Acts 16:14-15 we see Lydia exercising spiritual gifts within her own household and displaying hospitality (an excellent service) in the church. In Romans 16:1, Paul uses the exact title of Deacon to apply to Phoebe.

The New Testament evidence seems quite clear to Hurley and many others that the Bible allows for women to function in the office of Deacon or, at the very least, in a parallel and equal office of "Deaconess." Although the term Deaconess is never used in the New Testament, it did come into common use very soon thereafter in the early church.

What can we say in conclusion to the application of this principle from the Bible, particularly as it relates to denominations today? There are several smaller judicatories that allow women access to the office of Deacon – the Associate Reformed Presbyterians and the Reformed Presbyterian Church of North America (Covenanters). However, others, such as the Orthodox Presbyterians and the Presbyterian Church in America (PCA) do not.

Since the PCA Book of Church Order prohibits the ordaining of women as Deacons, no matter what individuals in the PCA may believe or interpret the Bible to teach (in that regard, no matter what a particular local church, or even Presbytery, might think), the Book of Church Order is based on the study and decision of many godly men, and we cannot lightly disregard it. This is an area that will be under discussion for many years to come in virtually every evangelical, Bible-believing denomination which views Deacons in the role of service rather than in a role of authority.

Just as we have taken all the study we have done so far in this series seriously, so must we take this issue seriously. And we must seek to keep that constant balance of which I have spoken several times already – that balance between seeking to understand what God wants us to do in the church, by way of government, and also keeping clear distinctions between issues that are not essential to salvation, that are not in and of themselves marks of the church. And as far as I am concerned, the issue of ordaining or not ordaining women to the office of Deacon falls into that latter category, and it is something that we should recognize as a tradition of the church which is probably best to follow at least for now.

CHAPTER 11

Qualifications for Office

In this chapter we will examine the Biblical qualifications for office as spelled out in the Bible. The subject matter is both so extensive and so important that this will be a double length chapter. But before we get into the list of specific qualifications, let me make some opening remarks by nature of ground rules for what will follow.

Kevin Reed, who is a Ruling Elder in a Presbyterian church, has written a brief contemporary monograph on the subject of Biblical church government. Mr. Reed most astutely points out (in a lengthy quote that is more than worthy of its space): "The scriptural mandates on the qualifications of the eldership require emphasis because they are often ignored in the church. An analogy to civil government may clarify the issue. In the civil government, [individuals] are not allowed to serve in an office unless they meet the prerequisites for that office. The qualifications for civil offices may be listed in the constitution of the nation (or state). For example, one qualification given for the President of the United States is that one must be at least 35 years old. The architects of the Constitution included this requirement to deter the hasty induction of political novices to the important office. No exceptions are made. No one may serve in the office unless they first fulfill the requirements. In civil government, it is easy to see the importance and function of qualifications for officers. Yet somehow, men balk at the idea of binding requirements in church government. It is as though the church's business is inferior to the role of the civil government. And it is as if the civil government has a more authoritative constitution than the one given by Christ (in the Bible) to the church." (*Biblical Church Government,* 1983, Presbyterian Heritage, Dallas).

Kevin Reed's point is well taken. The qualifications for church leaders are not just spelled out in the Bible as nice qualities that would be helpful if you saw one or two of them in a person before electing him to office. They are listed as necessities. In fact, in our key passage, 1 Timothy 3, at the beginning of the list of a number of important qualifications in verse 2, Paul writes: *"Therefore an overseer must be above reproach . . ."* Let me emphasize that word 'must.' It is a requirement. It is a command. These qualifications are necessary, not just nice.

My original impetus for writing this book was to provide some basic understanding to congregations on the nature of Presbyterian church government. This is especially needed in mission churches that are in the process of organizing. Drawing people from a wide variety of backgrounds, the very first thing that these young churches must do when they organize is to elect Elders and Deacons. And the decisions made at this time are the most important the church will ever make – because the church will seldom be any stronger than the original Elders. For those Elders are the ones who will make decisions that determine the future of the church, including to a large degree who the future Elders will be. And so electing Elders and Deacons in the church must never be viewed as just a popularity contest or who has the most experience or who knows the most Bible doctrine. Every qualification we will be looking at is important, and every candidate must be measured against the entire list.

Not that anyone will be found who measures up 100%. That kind of perfect person does not exist in the church of Jesus, except for the King and Head of the church Himself. I recall the first time I personally went through this list of 27 qualifications we are about to look at. It was during a brief interim pastorate I filled one summer while I was still a seminary student. I recall developing some method of objectifying these qualifications, and I came up with about a 60% score on my own test. I was almost ready to quit seminary. Except for the counsel of some godly Ruling Elders in that church, I just might have done so. In approaching this list of qualifications, we must keep a balance. They are impossible to measure up to perfectly, but they are at the same time necessary. With that balance in mind, let's see what they are.

We will be listing the requirements for both Elder and Deacon in one long list. I am doing this since the office of Deacon is an inclusive office. A church can function without Deacons, and in such a case the Elders are responsible for those tasks. And indeed, there are some similarities in the qualifications, which we will discuss at the appropriate point. But we will go through the list as one set of qualifications.

Also, with the exception of issues of ruling and teaching – the basic tasks for Elders we discussed in a previous unit of the series – each of the qualities listed here is also required for all Christians in general. These are character traits and Christian life actions that each believer should be seeking to develop and follow in his or her own life. The difference is that for Elders (and Deacons) in the church, these qualities must be exceptional, must be heightened, and must be clearly demonstrated.

In going through this list, we will follow the order as it appears in the Greek New Testament, which varies slightly with the King James Version. The translation of the Greek term will be given first as rendered by the KJV and then (if it is different) as rendered by the ESV, which is the translation of the Bible I have been using throughout this book.

The qualifications are listed for us in two chapters of the New Testament. Both are chapters that we have already looked at previously, 1 Timothy 3 and Titus 1. Recall that both of these books were written by Paul to his young apostolic assistants for the purpose of teaching them about organization of church government. And so it is fitting that each book contains extensive lists of qualifications for office.

Beginning in 1 Timothy 3:2, the first term listed is translated BLAMELESS in the KJV and ABOVE REPROACH in the ESV. In a sense this is an all-inclusive term and defines much of what follows in the list. It is a different word from that used in Titus 1:6, which is also translated into English as *"blameless."* The basic meaning here is that the person under consideration has no dominant sin or character traits that would disqualify him from office. There is nothing about this man's life or character that would be chargeable as sin or error or heresy. It does not mean perfection, for as we have already said, perfection is impossible in this life for any Christian, even for Elders.

The next term is translated in both the KJV and ESV the same way: HUSBAND OF ONE WIFE. The term appears both in 1 Timothy 3:2 in the list for Elder and in 1 Timothy 3:12 in the list for Deacon. As we discussed briefly in the previous chapter, the words used in the original Greek of the Scriptures imply much more than just a monogamous marriage. The underlying meaning is that of a "true husband," with all the Biblical injunctions for husbands in view. There are some who would say that this means that a person must be married in order to be an Elder or Deacon. But I doubt it. Certainly there were illustrations of Apostles in the New Testament who either were single or widowed, including Paul himself. So I don't believe we can say authoritatively that the Bible requires marriage. It only assumes it, since that is the normal pattern of life.

The issue here is one of holiness in all sexual and marriage matters. Certainly there cannot be the slightest hint of problem in this area of life for a man to function well as an Elder in the church. And yet it is one of the areas in which the strongest temptations, as well as falls into sin, frequently come, especially to Elders serving as Ministers of the Word. A church must exercise great care in examining a man in this qualification.

The next term on the list in verse 2 is translated either VIGILANT or SOBER-MINDED. I would probably prefer the translation "calm, cool, and collected." This same word is used in 1 Thessalonians 5:6 as the opposite of being asleep. I think we could best understand this qualification as the man's ability to deal with life situations in a wide-awake, eyes-open, realistic manner. Ready for whatever comes along. Not easily surprised. There is a sense of sharpness, of quickness, underlying this qualification. Certainly if an Elder in the church is surprised and shocked over and over again by what he confronts with the people, then his effectiveness will be greatly diminished, for he will have to spend far too much time overcoming the shock rather than dealing with the reality.

Next, appearing in both 1 Timothy 3:2 and in Titus 1:8 is the term SOBER or SELF-CONTROLLED. This is very similar to the term we just looked at. Perhaps it is more like our English word "sane." This requires that an Elder be in control of his wits – that he not be flighty or unrealistic about his role and duties in the church. The King James word SOBER does not relate to use of alcohol; that comes up a bit later. Rather, it is "sober-minded." I think you can see how an Elder who does not have good control of his emotions and his mental capacities would have great trouble functioning in his role.

Next on our list, this time appearing only in 1 Timothy 3:2, is the term OF GOOD BEHAVIOR or RESPECTABLE. Here I would opt for the translation "orderly." It means at its root someone whose life is well arranged. He is a respectable, honorable person. Everything about him is in good order. He is someone who keeps his promises. When he says he will take on a certain task in the church, you can depend on that task being accomplished. I believe this trait is one that covers what we today would think of as good management techniques – the ability to do time management, to delegate authority, to exercise leadership and responsibility without always having to do everything yourself.

Our next qualification is translated the same way in both the KJV and in the ESV, and in almost every other translation for that matter. This is the qualification of HOSPITABLE. The item appears in both lists for Elders – 1 Timothy 3:2 and Titus 1:8. It is clearly a very important qualification.

To be hospitable means that an Elder must be generous and kind to all people. He must not only have a number of close friends in the church; his friends must include outsiders. And in making friends with outsiders, it is important to note that you have to meet people on the level where they are, and not where you are. It is very easy for a devout, pious, godly man to live in a very tight inner circle and really associate only with people who believe like he does, act like he does, almost look like he does. The qualification of hospitality means an Elder must break out of this mold. It is not enough just to get along; an Elder must be open. Certainly this hospitality could – and I believe should – result in his opening not only his life, but also his home – to have people visit for friendship and to have their needs met. The qualification of hospitality may be one of the most neglected areas in the life of many churches today, and one that I believe we must pay more attention to in the future.

The next item on our list is APT TO TEACH or ABLE TO TEACH. It also appears in both Elders' lists in 1 Timothy and in Titus. We talked about teaching at great length in an earlier chapter on the tasks of Elders, but let's just review a few of the high points. The qualification of teaching does not imply that every Elder must be a gifted, professional, classroom-style teacher. But he certainly must have a proven ability to communicate the truth of the Bible to others. Remember that key verse we have looked at several times in Ephesians 4:12? It reads in part that the task of a Pastor-Teacher – of every Elder – is to *"equip the saints for the work of ministry."* Surely this equipping will require the passing on of basic content and doctrine from the Bible to others and to pass it on in a practical, usable way.

Remember, the authority of any church officer is not who he is, but rather is the Word of God. An Elder does not need some sort of "authoritative" teaching gift. He just needs to know the Bible and to teach its principles and application to others.

The next qualification is one that appears in three places, which makes it both unique and important. It is on the list for Elders and the list for Deacons in 1 Timothy 3 and is also on the list for Elders in Titus 1. This is the qualification that says that a church officer must NOT BE GIVEN TO WINE, or to add one additional word, as the NIV does: NOT GIVEN TO MUCH WINE. The ESV renders it as NOT A DRUNKARD.

This phrase could be more literally translated as "not one who lingers besides his wine." If you follow this literal translation, then it is clear that the Bible here is not dealing with the use of alcoholic beverages, but rather with their abuse or addiction. However, we cannot leave the issue with just this simple comment because there is a great need for balance on this issue in the church today, and in some quarters this subject will generate more heat than it will light.

There are several Presbyterian denominations that will not allow the use of alcoholic beverages for their officers, such as the Reformed Presbyterian Church, General Synod (commonly known as the Covenanters). This was a hallmark of the old Bible Presbyterian Church. In fact, it was one of the key issues that brought about the separation of that body from the Orthodox

Presbyterian Church in the late 1930s. With many of the former Bible Presbyterians now having entered into the PCA through the "Joining and Receiving" with the Reformed Presbyterian Church, Evangelical Synod several decades ago, the issue is very much a live one in the PCA. In fact, several times in the denomination's history overtures have come up from presbyteries seeking to have the church declare a position of total abstinence as a requirement for its church officers.

The Presbyterian Church in America, along with most of the smaller evangelical Presbyterian denominations, refused to make this a requirement for office. In other words, in the PCA it is not to be a requirement that church officers must take vows of total abstinence. However, there are a number of local churches where this view is strongly held, and in such cases it is important to proceed with great caution and care in the application of this Biblical qualification. While it is true that the Bible does not demand total abstinence on its list of qualifications, in some local situations it may be the wisest course of action to apply that standard, understanding that it is an important sociological and cultural issue in the United States today.

I will assume that no one reading this book needs to be reminded of the great damage that alcoholism – alcohol abuse – has caused in our nation and in our churches. In fact, this issue could and should be properly broadened to include drugs other than alcohol. Even if a church decides that total abstinence is not to be a requirement for church office, it is important that every Elder be ready to proclaim the truth of the Bible to show to the church and to the world that there is indeed a serious problem in our society and that faith in Jesus Christ and following his word is the very best way to resolve this problem in anyone's life.

The next several terms which appear in 1 Timothy 3:3 and, in the case of the first one, also in Titus 1:7, return us to issues of character, of attitudes. The first is translated NO STRIKER or NOT VIOLENT. The issue here is that an Elder should not be a bully – should not be pugnacious. This term describes a person who always walks around with a chip on his shoulder. I hope it is obvious that an Elder should be just the opposite; he should be one who is committed to settle disputes rather than start them.

The next term is PATIENT or GENTLE. This is not the same term that appears in the list of the fruit of the Spirit in Galatians 5:22-23, but it is somewhat similar. It could probably also be translated as moderate, yielding, kind, or genial. I believe you see the implications.

Actually the next term is very similar. Translated by the KJV as NOT A BRAWLER and in the ESV as NOT QUARRELSOME, it describes someone who is not easily involved in fighting or strife. It comes from the same root word in the Greek from which the noun "sword" is taken. As you can see, all three of these previous terms are very similar.

Out next qualification is NOT COVETOUS or NOT A LOVER OF MONEY. There is another item on the list for Deacons in 1 Timothy 3:8 and also on the list for Elders in Titus 1:8 that seems on the surface to be similar but has a different emphasis. This term is best understood in light of the Tenth Commandment's indictment against wanting something that belongs to another person, whatever that might be. Covetousness is a deadly sin, and to find that sin in the life of a man who aspires to become, or who already is, an Elder can bring great damage to the church of Jesus Christ. Elders are in offices that grant to them a position of special trust, and anyone who uses that trust to take advantage of someone or something else in order to feed his own lusts and desires of covetousness is clearly disqualified from service.

Next is one more item that appears in all three lists. And this qualification requires that a church officer RULE WELL his OWN HOUSE or, to use the ESV translation, MANAGES his OWN HOUSEHOLD WELL.

In a very real sense, this is the task of ruling we discussed in an earlier unit, but it is not simply a task. It is also a qualification for office, even for the office of Deacon. Recall that Deacons do not exercise oversight. They do not rule in the church. It is important that when Paul mentions this qualification in 1 Timothy 3:4 in the case of Elders, he then makes the analogy to ruling in the church in verse 5. But in the list of qualifications for Deacon, Paul only mentions the basic fact in verse 12; he does not make the same analogy to rule in the church. This is because Deacons do not rule; they serve.

But this does not mean that the issue of a man's relationship to his family is not important. Even a Deacon must pass the qualification of managing his own family well. I believe that this managing of one's own family entails at least three different areas. First, a man must be in a Biblical relationship with his wife, in terms of loving his wife and in terms of her being in subjection to his headship.

Second, the man must be in a Biblical relationship with his children, requiring obedience and practicing discipline. In this regard we must look at the slightly different way Paul presents this qualification in the list in Titus 1:6. This verse reads: *". . . above reproach, the husband of one wife, and his children are believers and not open to the charge of debauchery or insubordination."*

I believe the issue of obedience and discipline for the children is clear enough, but what do we make of this requirement of having children who believe? Must it be a pre-requisite that every church officer, if he has children, can serve in office only if his children are faithful, practicing Christians? If this were indeed the case, then many, many thousands of Elders and Deacons – even Ministers of the Word – both today and throughout church history would have been disqualified for service. This would be a very literal and a very narrow interpretation of what Paul has in mind.

Rather, I believe the issue is that they live in the household of the prospective officer as covenant children. They are baptized; they are under the preaching of the Word; they are brought up in the nurture and admonition of the Lord. They should, in fact, be treated as Christian children. But what happens to them after they become adults and leave the home? What their ultimate, personal standing with God in his eternal kingdom might or might not be is not, to my way of thinking, the issue. No father is totally responsible for the salvation of his own children. That is a function of the electing grace of a sovereign God. A father must do everything within his possibility to apply the means of grace to the life of the child while he or she is in the home. But the ultimate destiny of the child is not up to the father; it is up to God. To apply so narrow an interpretation of this verse as to

132

eliminate from eligibility for office any man whose child turns out not to follow after Jesus as an adult is going beyond the reasonable limits of Scripture.

There is a third area in which managing one's own family well has application, and that is that the officer must be in full Biblical relationship with all household matters. He must manage not only the people, but also everything else under his control and his responsibility.

Let's turn now to the next item on our list. It appears only once, in 1 Timothy 3:6. This is the issue of the officer not being a NOVICE or a RECENT CONVERT. The issue here is not simply one of chronological age, but rather of age in the faith. Recall that in the next chapter, at 4:12, Paul tells his obviously young associate, *"Let no one despise you for your youth . . ."* You see, Timothy was a very young man, most likely in his early 20's. But he certainly was fully qualified, Biblically, to be an officer in the church. So the issue is not chronological age, but faith age. How long has the person been a Christian?

I believe it can, and frequently does, bring untold harm to elevate to office in the church a man who, although mature in age, is new to the Christian faith. He may be a great leader in the secular world, but time must be taken for the people of God to see him work out his faith in the context of the church and of the world, probably for a number of years. We in America have been quite guilty of pushing famous people who become Christians later in their lives into positions of leadership in the church. This is not a good idea; it is contrary to God's instructions for church officers.

The next item on the list is in 3:7: HAVE A GOOD REPORT or BE WELL THOUGHT OF BY OUTSIDERS. As the ESV rendering emphasizes, this reputation is to be outside the church, among non-Christians. Especially must this be true not only in matters of material and financial matters; it should include every aspect of relationships. A man whose business or personal finances are in question in the world certainly should be looked at very closely, if at all, before being given an office in the church.

The next two items are only listed in Paul's section concerning qualifications for Deacons. The first of these is GRAVE or DIGNIFIED. I prefer the ESV translation. The issue at hand here really is one of respect. Perhaps we could call this term 'serious'.

The second of these "Deacon-only" qualifications is NOT DOUBLE-TONGUED. This qualification concerns consistency. This means that the candidate for office must be a man who tells everyone the same story. We will hold our special discussion concerning items that are listed for Deacons only until we look at the other two in just a moment.

First there is a qualification on the list that is not only in the section for Deacons in 1 Timothy 3, but is also on the list for Elders in Titus 1. And this is one to which we had referred a bit earlier: NOT GREEDY OF FILTHY LUCRE to use the KJV language or, in more contemporary language, NOT GREEDY FOR DISHONEST GAIN. The issue here is that an Elder, or a Deacon for that matter, should not use his position of leadership, his office in the church, as a place to enhance and improve his own economic position. Sometimes you hear people speak of those who "join the right church" for political or business reasons.

I personally know of an example in a large city on the East Coast of the United States where a man moved his membership from a conservative, Bible-believing church, which was small and not particularly influential, to a much larger, more affluent mainline, liberal church and then two months later ran for and was elected to the city government. This man could not have become mayor, he obviously thought, if he was the member of the wrong church. Well, if a man has this attitude, this point would most surely disqualify him from office in the church.

The next two items, which appear in 1 Timothy 3:9-10, are on the list for Deacons only. The first of these is translated two different ways: HOLDING THE MYSTERY OF FAITH IN PURE CONSCIENCE in the KJV and WITH A CLEAR CONSCIENCE in the ESV. This qualification speaks of a man's attitude in his own heart toward religion. No matter what he might say with his lips, he must believe these truths personally. He must not be a theological hypocrite. I think it is important to note that this qualification makes it crystal clear that even though Deacons are not involved in teaching and ruling in the church, they still must stand up to theological scrutiny. They cannot believe something other than the standards of the church and still be elected to office.

Next is the issue that the Deacon must FIRST BE PROVEN or TESTED. This is very similar to the issue we looked at earlier on our list concerning Elders – that they not be novices, that they not be new to the faith. Before a man can be elevated to any office in the church, there must be a period of time in which his experience in church matters can be proven and tested.

One way to do this is to have men who are potential candidates for office serve in various capacities in the church. Potential Elders could be involved in teaching somewhere in the church. Potential Deacons could serve on building or finance committees or could get involved in some sort of outreach program to help people in the neighborhood. There are many practical ways to test a man's gifts in the church.

Also, I believe this qualification gives us the responsibility to conduct some training classes for officers prior to their nomination and election. In these classes the duties, the tasks, the function of the office can be discussed, both theoretically and practically, and various items of doctrine and polity can be covered to ensure that there is agreement to the teachings of the church. A few churches even require that potential officers pass tests covering basic principles of Bible knowledge and doctrinal truths.

We want to pause for just a moment now to see if these four items which appear only on the list of qualifications for Deacon were in some way unique or different from those on the lists for Elder. And I believe our clear conclusion is that they are not. In fact, they are in many ways very similar to items already covered. *"First be tested"* is very much like *"not a novice."* *"Worthy of respect"* and *"dignified"* are also very, very similar.

I believe we can come to the conclusion that the items on the list for Deacon which are listed only there are so much like the rest of the qualifications that there is no need to separate them out and make a special list just for this office. Again, with the exception of the issues of ruling and teaching, which apply only to the office of Elder, all the rest of these qualifications are important and could be properly applied to men who become candidates for Deacon as well as Elder.

Continuing now with items that appear only in the list given in Titus 1, we find the English word BLAMELESS (ABOVE REPROACH in the ESV) again in verse 6. This is a different word from that one we saw earlier in 1 Timothy 3:2. The picture here is a man with an irreproachable character. You look at this man's life, and you can see nothing in his character, in his life style or in his personality that would disqualify him from office. Again, it does not mean or demand perfection, but it does mean he stands out above most men in his character traits – enough so as to be clearly noticeable.

Next we have NOT SELF-WILLED or NOT AROGANT. The issue here is not so much selfishness as it is self-pleasing. Especially this term speaks to involvement in worldly matters. Some people try to separate their life – compartmentalize it if you will – so that they can be religious when it is important; but in order to satisfy their own desires and lusts, they carry on in the world as if they were not in fact separate from the world. They want the pleasure of this life, while at the same time they want the security of eternal life. Well, if a man has this self-pleasing idea about the church and about religion, then he has no business being elected to an office of leadership in the church.

The next item is NOT SOON ANGRY or NOT QUICK-TEMPERED. It is very similar to one we looked at earlier also. The person in view here is someone who is not trigger-tempered. Not that there is anything inherently wrong with anger. There is a time for proper, Biblically based anger. But it should never come quickly. There is the need for the gift of long-suffering in the character of every church office. People frequently will do something or say something that, if reacted to too quickly, would result in problems. No, a church officer must be very patient in these matters.

Next is LOVER OF GOOD MEN or, as the ESV puts it, leaving out the personal application, LOVER OF GOOD. Actually, the word "men" does not appear in the Greek, and so the ESV is the better translation. This means that a church officer should be ready to do that which is beneficial to others. And, after all, isn't that the very nature of Biblical love – always putting the well being of others ahead of yourself. Certainly Elders (and Deacons, who deal with people in need) should exemplify this characteristic.

Next is the word JUST or UPRIGHT. This word does not refer to "justification." It has nothing to do with a man's standing before God. Rather, it speaks to the issue of fair dealings – of being the sort of person who would have the qualities of a good judge. Many times church officers are put in a position to make judgments. Sometimes Elders serve officially on ecclesiastical courts, and they in fact are acting just like judges. Surely this is a needed characteristic.

Next is the word HOLY. This qualification describes the officer's attitude towards God. This means that he is living a life which can be referred to as holy, or separated to the work and will of God – that his life is not just dedicated to fulfilling his own and his family's needs, as important as they are, but rather his life is truly dedicated to seeing that the will of God is carried out

– in the home, in the church, and in the world.

Finally on our list is the term TEMPERATE or DISCIPLINED. This word is the only one in our list which also appears in the list Paul gives in Galatians 5:22-23 of the fruit of the Spirit. There it is usually translated SELF-CONTROL. This refers to matters of general discipline in a man's life. There should be discipline in everything – in the use of alcohol and drugs, in the use of food (excessive obesity would be a sign of lack of self-control), discipline in matters of personal health. Whatever we do in life that needs balance, that needs discipline, in those areas the potential church officer should be known for his discipline and self-control.

This completes our list of qualifications for office in the church. And once again we must remind ourselves that if we had to measure up perfectly to every one of these items, no one would be found fit for service. But certainly some are fit. God intended for his church to have leaders, to have officers. And so it is the responsibility of the people of God to examine all candidates – Teaching or Ruling Elders and Deacons – and apply this list of qualifications for office to them before they are elected to serve. For only if these standards are maintained can the church have any hope of maintaining strong, godly leaders to guide and direct its affairs and its work. And remember the point on which we began this chapter. These qualifications are necessary, not just nice.

CHAPTER 12:

The Connectional and Confessional Nature of the Church

In this final chapter I want to cover two separate items. The first concerns the connectional nature of Presbyterian church government. The second is the confessional nature of that government. The reasons for putting these two items together are twofold. Biblically speaking, both issues stem from the same basic passage of Scripture, the story of the meeting of the Jerusalem Council in Acts 15. The secondary reason is that Ruling Elder Kevin Reed included them so effectively in his monograph (which I referenced in the last chapter). Reed's booklet (now out of print but available on CD through Still Water Revival Books) was one of my inspirations to begin work on this larger, but equally basic work.

While we have stressed so far the fact that Presbyterian church government is the rule and leadership in the church by a plurality of Elders in each congregation, there is something else that is unique to Presbyterianism as well. In fact, it is possible to have rule by Elders practiced on the local church level (I am aware of some Baptist and independent churches that do just this) and yet not be Presbyterian. For what makes a church truly

Presbyterian is that, in addition to local rule by Elders, it also has a system of government by graded courts of the church. These courts meet at different levels, but the basic principles are the same. Each court has its own administrative and judicial responsibility. But the lower court always has the right of appeal of a decision, either administrative or judicial, to a higher court.

As I mentioned, the basic text to show this principle from the Bible is Acts 15. I don't want to take the time to go over the entire chapter, but let's set the stage and get the context at least by beginning with verses 1 through 6: " *But some men came down from Judea and were teaching the brothers, "Unless you are circumcised according to the custom of Moses, you cannot be saved." [2] And after Paul and Barnabas had no small dissension and debate with them, Paul and Barnabas and some of the others were appointed to go up to Jerusalem to the apostles and the elders about this question. [3] So, being sent on their way by the church, they passed through both Phoenicia and Samaria, describing in detail the conversion of the Gentiles, and brought great joy to all the brothers. [4] When they came to Jerusalem, they were welcomed by the church and the apostles and the elders, and they declared all that God had done with them. [5] But some believers who belonged to the party of the Pharisees rose up and said, "It is necessary to circumcise them and to order them to keep the law of Moses." [6] The apostles and the elders were gathered together to consider this matter."*

There are several important points to be made right in these early verses of the chapter. To begin with, a dispute about certain teaching in the church arose in a particular, local church in the town of Antioch. As interesting and important as the dispute is, the subject matter is not our concern at this point. What is clear from the passage is that the dispute was not settled in the local church in Antioch. They decided to seek the advice of a broader group of churchmen and appointed Paul and Barnabas to go to Jerusalem to meet with this group. Sometimes, especially in smaller churches, it is impossible to settle deep differences at the local level.

The next important point to make is that this group, this assembly, met publicly to debate the issue. Clearly both sides of the issue were represented. While it does not say so explicitly, it is my impression that as Paul and Barnabas traveled on the way to Jerusalem and discussed these issues with other believers in churches along the way, representatives from these churches also came to the meeting. Surely this was an important issue.

And in the debate in the assembly, the dispute is ultimately settled – not by the church where it began, but rather by another, external group of Elders. Recall we had pointed out earlier in the book that in this case the Apostles were functioning as Elders, not in their specialized role as Apostles.

Skipping over the content of the debate itself, looking down to verses 23 through 29, we see that ultimately the assembly pronounced a decision which was clearly understood by all present to be the will of God in the matter: *". . . The brothers, both the apostles and the elders, to the brothers who are of the Gentiles in Antioch and Syria and Cilicia, greetings. [24] Since we have heard that some persons have gone out from us and troubled you with words, unsettling your minds, although we gave them no instructions, [25] it has seemed good to us, having come to one accord, to choose men and send them to you with our beloved*

Barnabas and Paul, [26] men who have risked their lives for the sake of our Lord Jesus Christ. [27] We have therefore sent Judas and Silas, who themselves will tell you the same things by word of mouth. [28] For it has seemed good to the Holy Spirit and to us to lay on you no greater burden than these requirements: [29] that you abstain from what has been sacrificed to idols, and from blood, and from what has been strangled, and from sexual immorality. If you keep yourselves from these, you will do well. Farewell."

And finally we see that this letter, which contained the decision of the council, was authoritative. In fact it required submission of churches other than even Antioch, from where the question initially arose. In Acts 16:4 we see Paul and Silas delivering this decision of the Jerusalem Council to all the churches they were visiting on their journey.

This is the essence of the connectional nature of Presbyterian church government. An issue – an important administrative or judicial issue – that cannot be settled or carried out on the local church level can and should be sent to a higher court for a judgment by other Elders outside the local church. Certainly we see that this issue was not something unique to a single congregation that could have been settled only there. Rather, this issue dealt with basic issues of principle that had application far beyond the local church in which they first came to light. And notice also that the decree – the decision – contained commands. This was not just pious advice, not simply a recommendation that would be nice to be followed. There was such a connectional relationship between these churches and the council that the churches understood their need to submit to the command – the rule – of the council.

It is very important that we notice this is not something that is part of the revelatory nature of the Bible. This is not God's way of bringing about some new, special revelation. Notice that throughout every stage of discussion and decision-making process, the Elders were clearly in view. This is not Apostles exercising apostolic gifts. This is Elders functioning in the role of church leadership.

This pattern of Elders functioning in leadership continues throughout the book of Acts. Just before his arrest in Jerusalem, in Acts 21, verses 17-19, Paul meets with the Elders in the Jerusalem church and, in describing his missionary journey, speaks in terms of his eldership: *"When we had come to Jerusalem, the brothers received us gladly. [18] On the following day Paul went in with us to James, and all the elders were present. [19] After greeting them, he related one by one the things that God had done among the Gentiles through his ministry."*

Now, how does this principle of connectionalism that we see taught in Acts 15 work out in Presbyterian church government? Well, the basic principle is that the local church must have at least one level of appeal – one higher court to which to turn. Depending on the country in which you find the churches, the number of churches, and the location of the churches, you may find more than two levels. You may find three levels as you have in the PCA and OPC – the local church, the Presbytery, and the General Assembly. You may even find four levels in some larger denominations, adding what is called a regional synod between the level of Presbytery and General Assembly. It is not crucial to determine how many levels there are. I personally believe that the fewer the better. But what is important to note is that to be truly Presbyterian, there must be this level of connectionalism.

What is it the courts do at each level of this connectional system? Let's examine the three-tier system and look at each court level briefly. On the local church level, the group of Elders is known as the Session. We have already discussed all the various issues that the Session might be involved in, such as preaching, education, music, sacraments, finances, admonishment (all of these being more or less administrative in nature) and then, of course, the judicial processes that stem from church discipline.

How about the Presbytery level? Well, anything administrative that can be done more practically on a regional level is well put into their hands – such as sponsoring youth camps, special retreats and training projects, doing church planting work in the region, and so forth. The most important work that the Presbytery performs is that of examining, approving, and ordaining men who are seeking to become Teaching Elders in the denomination. We need to spend just a moment on this very special issue.

When we examine the New Testament evidence, it quickly becomes clear that there was a special procedure developed early in the history of the church to designate those men who were to serve in leadership offices in the church. This process has come to be known today as "ordination."

We have already seen this occur in Acts 6 with the origin of the office of Deacon. There, after the Seven were selected by the congregation, they were presented to the Apostles (functioning, you will recall, as Elders), who then proceeded to the ceremony, which involved prayer and the laying on of hands. This is the essence of the act of ordination.

Looking at the key book that we have been examining all along, 1 Timothy, in Chapter 4, verse 14, we find an account of Timothy's own ordination. Paul writes: *"Do not neglect the gift you have, which was given you by prophecy when the council of elders laid their hands on you."* Setting aside the issue about the special, prophetic gift that Timothy was given (recall that we see him in the special, temporary office of Evangelist and thus having such special gifts), the issue we want to focus on is the process – the act – of ordination. Again, it involved the laying on of hands. And who is the group in view in this process? The "council [or body] of Elders" or, in our Presbyterian tradition, the Presbytery.

Now, our first assumption is that this council of Elders is not made up only of men in a local church situation (the Session of the local church) but rather involves a broader grouping, such as a regional body – a Presbytery. In Timothy's case it clearly appears to be the latter. According to 2 Timothy 1:6, Paul participated in Timothy's ordination. He was a part of the group involved. However, this evidence is not in and of itself conclusive. So this is an area that can, and has been, properly left to good judgment and tradition in the church.

The normal pattern is that in the local church situation, where Deacons and Elders are selected from within members of the local congregation, the ordination is left to the Elders in the local church – the Session. One frequent exception to this is when a new church is organized. Following the pattern set forth in Titus 1:5, one Presbyter (Elder), presumably given some special authority to act on behalf of the larger body, is given the responsibility of singly ordaining the original Elders in a church. Apart from this exception, the normal, Biblical practice is that ordination should be the act of a group of Elders.

The pattern of holding the ordination of Teaching Elders at the level of the Presbytery is an important one as well, and leads us back to our discussion of the responsibility of the second level of courts in a connectional system. This is probably the most important thing that a Presbytery does. Because of the need for continuity in theology and church polity background and training, leaving the responsibility for education, examination, and ultimate approval of ordination in the hands of a regional body made up of a number of both Teaching and Ruling Elders appears to continue to be the best course of action to provide for a continuing supply of educated clergy in the church.

However the process takes place, the important point is that no man should take an office to himself. In this day and age – with a growing number of people entering into various forms of independent ministries, without having to answer to any discipline or authority in the church – the system of ordination by Presbytery appears to give the greatest degree of safety to the church.

If there is yet a third level of church court, such as a General Assembly, this is most logically set up within the bounds of a separate country or nation. At this level some of the functions that can be assigned to the General Assembly include the oversight of all foreign missions programs, the production of education curriculums, and the development and control of educational institutions. Also, such a court would serve as the place of final appeal in all judicial cases that cannot be settled at a lower level – sort of a supreme court. This would then follow the pattern of the Jerusalem Council that we examined earlier in Acts 15.

Next we want to turn our attention to consider the confessional nature of Presbyterian church government. And this point builds on the Jerusalem Council passage in Acts as well. Recall that the decision of this council had a binding nature within the churches. The pronouncement did two things. It declared the teaching of the Judaizers as heresy, and it also gave instructions to members of the church concerning certain practices in the life of the congregations. In a sense, this edict was the first truly Christian "confessional document."

Elsewhere in the Bible we see the same concept developing further. In his first epistle, the Apostle John sets forth several tests of true faith and doctrine. This is clearest in Chapter 4, verses 1-3: *"Beloved, do not believe every spirit, but test the spirits to see whether they are from God, for many false prophets have gone out into the world. [2] By this you know the Spirit of God: every spirit that confesses that Jesus Christ has come in the flesh is from God, [3] and every spirit that does not confess Jesus is not from God. This is the spirit of the antichrist, which you heard was coming and now is in the world already."* Again we have the beginning of confessional statements by which truth can be separated from heresy.

In the early days of church history, several confessional statements were developed by the church for the same reasons. Some of these are in very common use today, such as the Apostles' Creed, the Nicene Creed, and others. The works of several later councils, such as the Council of Chalcedon, made even more extensive statements that then were used to guide the church for years to come.

At the time of the Reformation, there was such a need for reform and renewal in the church that most of the protesting groups of Christians (the Protestants) adopted their own confessional standards, showing at the same time how they were true to the Scriptures and different from Roman Catholicism.

In the Presbyterian tradition, the most important of these documents is known as the Westminster Standards, which include the Confession of Faith, the Larger Catechism, and the Shorter Catechism. All three of these documents form the constitution of the Presbyterian Church in America, as well as a number of other Biblically based Presbyterian denominations.

These confessional documents have several real values today. They are far more than just historical documents. They are in fact objective standards by which officers in the church can test all teaching and all teachers that come into the church. This serves to help protect the church from man's constant desire to use only subjective, emotional, inward impulses to interpret Scripture. People are constantly seeking to come to their own personal understanding of the Word of God. If left to do this without any checks and balances, the effect of sin will lead everyone astray into error and heresy sooner or later.

But the confessional nature of the church provides a tremendous safeguard against such impulses and errors. That is why each officer in the church, including Elders and Deacons ordained at the local church level, as well as Teaching Elders ordained at the Presbytery level, is bound by vows to uphold the beliefs of his church and to work to protect these standards from dilution and needless change.

This brings to a end this chapter on connectionalism and confessionalism – in fact, a conclusion to the book on church government. Let me return to the point with which I began this work. Recall we saw that God used human leaders in his church to bring blessings to his people – to provide ministry and form and order to the work of the Kingdom of God on earth. Jesus' work centered on the training of leaders. The New Testament epistles are, to a great extent, manuals of leadership training or accounts of the life and ministry of leaders.

And we have seen that the key office of leadership in the church, exercising ruling and teaching functions, is the office of Elder, ably assisted in performing ministries of service by the office of Deacon, and that these two offices are the only continuing offices in the church today.

My prayer is that the reader – especially those of you who are learning about the Presbyterian form of government for the first time – may understand why we who practice our church government as Presbyterians believe it is so important to practice these biblical principles as closely as possible. I suspect that other forms of government might work more efficiently, but I sincerely doubt if any other form of government can claim to be more biblically based. May the head of our Church, even Jesus the Lord, be blest as we seek to follow his methods of carrying out his office as a King.

If you have enjoyed and profited from this book and would like to order additional copies, they are available directly from the Publisher.

Since the book is well suited for distribution to new members of both organized churches and (especially) start-up church plants, there are special rates for bulk orders (to the same address). Bookstores and church sponsored book tables may take advantage of the same prices for outright purchases (returnable orders will be at the standard 40% discount rates).

Single copy	$12.00 each
10 or more copies	$11.00 each
25 or more copies	$10.00 each
50 or more copies	$8.00 each
100 or more copies	$6.00 each

(Orders of 200 or more copies should contact Metokos Press for special print run pricing.)

A 15% shipping and handling fee will be added to orders of less than 50; 10% for orders of 50 or more.

Send check or money order to

Metokos Press
211 Main Street, Suite 108
Narrows, VA 24124

Or order online with a credit card at

www.metokos.org/press

About the Author

Dr. Clements was ordained in July of 1974 in the National Presbyterian Church (the original name of the PCA). After several years as a pastor in Central Georgia Presbytery, he returned to the U. S. Navy where he had previously spent 12 years on active duty prior to entering seminary. Having left as an enlisted man (Chief Petty Officer), he returned as a Navy Chaplain.

Serving ten additional years on active duty on assignments with Destroyer Squadrons in San Diego; at the Naval Air Station in Pensacola; as Chaplain for a nuclear-powered guided missile cruiser and a submarine tender in Norfolk, and finally as Chaplain of the Naval Hospital, Newport, RI, Don retired in 1985.

For the next 18 years he pastored two 'turn-around' church revitalizations of small churches in Blacksburg and Narrows, VA. On January 1st, 2003 he moved full time into a ministry he had developed called *Metokos Ministries – Encouragement for Small Churches.* Affiliated with the Presbyterian Evangelistic Fellowship (PEF) as an Evangelist, Don works with small churches (mostly under 100 members) that need encouragement and resources to develop Vision Plans, go through Pulpit Committee transitions, and other specific needs.

Don holds an MDiv (with honors) from Covenant Theological Seminary in St. Louis, and a DMin (in Adult Education) from Gordon Conwell Theological Seminary in South Hamilton, MA. He and his wife, Esther, live with their Cocker Spaniel 'Shadow' in their newly remodeled retirement home in the Appalachian Mountain town of Narrows, Virginia and they spend lots of time visiting their three grown daughters who currently live in Mississippi, South Dakota, and Virginia.